tortoise

understanding and caring for your pet

Written by
Lance Jepson MA VetMB CBiol MSB MRCVS

tortoise

understanding and
caring for your pet

Written by
Lance Jepson MA VetMB CBiol MSB MRCVS

Magnet & Steel Ltd

www.magnetsteel.com

Printed and bound in South Korea.

ISBN: 978-1-907337-14-7
ISBN: 1-907337-14-8

Contents

Introduction 08

Tortoises & us 10

Species & varieties 18

Hermann's Tortoise 20
Western Hermann's Tortoise 23
Eastern Hermann's Tortoise 24
Spur-thighed Tortoise (Testudo graeca) Complex 30
Spur-thighed Tortoise 32
Spur-thighed or Greek Tortoise 34
Turkish Spur-thighed Tortoise 38
Spur-thighed Tortoise Testudo graeca zarudnyi 40
Tunisian Tortoise 44
Marginated Tortoises 46
Horsfield's or Russian Tortoise 48

Aspects of tortoise biology & behaviour 52

Senses 58

Behaviour 62

Sociability 64

Hatchlings & young tortoises 68

The importance of sunlight 70

Acquiring a tortoise 78

How to spot a healthy tortoise 82

Housing 90

Vivaria 92

Heat	94
Lighting	96
A tortoise kitchen	110
Hibernation	132
Making more tortoises	152
Reproduction: related problems	168
In sickness & in health	172
More information	190
Further reading	191
Weights & measures	192

Introduction

In recent years the idea of keeping
tortoises as pets has once again become
popular after a couple of decades of their
comparative unavailability. Truth to tell
tortoises never fell out of favour - it was the
necessity of the importation ban of these
tortoises into Europe, including the United
Kingdom, that caused their unavailability,
but the situation has now changed.

How have things altered? Well, nearly thirty years
have elapsed since the ban and we now know so
much more about tortoise needs and husbandry
requirements. In addition the keeping of reptiles
as pets is now booming and this has fuelled the
development of a wide range of reptile-keeping
products that make tortoise care so much easier
and more rewarding. Both of these factors have
meant that captive breeding of many tortoise species
has become almost commonplace, to the extent that
significant numbers of captive-bred tortoises are
now available through specialist pet shops and
private breeders.

This book will concentrate on the three most common Eurasian tortoises – the spur-thigh tortoise (Testudo graeca), Hermann's tortoise (T. hermanni) and Horsfield's tortoise (T. horsfieldi). These three species make up the bulk of the European chelonian pet trade, although other related tortoises will be mentioned for completeness.

I hope that this book will help you learn the basics of how to look after your tortoise. Your tortoise should have a long and happy life and reward you with a relationship that could conceivably last your life-time and extend into that of your children. What other pet can offer you that?

Tortoises & us

Tortoises have been around a long time and, with their peculiar looks and perceived longevity relative to our own, it's not surprising that they have not only come to the attention of people of all ages and continents, but they have also entered into our mythology too.

In many myths tortoises are portrayed as celestial Atlas-like supporters of our planet. In China the tortoise represents the Great Triad with the sky the dome of its carapace, the earth its plastron whilst the atmosphere is the body of the tortoise sandwiched between. The four feet are the four corners of the earth. In Japan it supports the Cosmic Mountain with its home of the Immortals. The Hindu god Vishnu descended to earth as Kurma, the tortoise and dived beneath the waters to hold up Mount Mandara and thereby underpin India.

Children often find tortoises fascinating, but interactions should be monitored and hands washed afterwards!

Another Indian myth details how Chukwa the tortoise supports the elephant Maha-pudma who himself supports the world. Mongols, Balinese and Amerindians all have their legend-equivalents involving tortoises. It is little wonder that Terry Pratchett invented a similar mythology for his fictional Discworld novels. Here the Great A'Tuin (admittedly a turtle, not a tortoise) sails through the universe with four elephants stood upon his carapace to bear the Discworld above their heads.

Chinese legends list the tortoise as one of the Four Spiritually Endowed Creatures, along with the dragon, the phoenix and the qilin (an odd, at times unicorn-like mythological beast). The tortoise represents the water element and is the passive, feminine and negative yin to the universe's yang. It is also a sign of longevity, strength and endurance and when combined with the dragon it becomes a symbol of invincibility.

Tortoises have not only been mythologised, sadly they have been exploited too. Tortoises have been cooked and eaten and their shells used as objects of decoration wherever they are found. The Ancient Greeks made lyres from tortoises, the empty shell acting as the soundbox. However it is as a pet that the tortoise was most abused in Europe. Over the centuries there had been a steady trickle of pet tortoises into northern European countries.

Pictured:
Today we know not
to feed just lettuce.

In its correspondence column, The Girl's Own Paper of May 1st 1880 the editor gives the following answer, "You do not state what kind of tortoises yours are. If the common, they will live in the garden, and eat vegetables." Sadly, some 230 years later, many people seem to still believe that this is the sum of all tortoise knowledge.

As their popularity increased, that trickle of tortoises became a flood. In the early twentieth century Mediterranean species began to be imported into Great Britain in their thousands and it is estimated that over ten million tortoises were imported into the UK alone in the century prior to the 1984 ban. Often loaded as live ballast, the act of transportation gave rise to massive numbers of mortalities and serious injuries. Tortoises were regarded as cheap and disposable, along with another pet that deserved better – the goldfish. Prices of between sixpence (2.5 pence) and a shilling (5 pence) were common. Over two million were imported in 1938, the same year that veterinarian Frederick Hobday, the then president of the Universities Federation for Animal Welfare (UFAW) sent a letter to The Times (dated 6th December) stating that only 1 or 2 per cent of imported tortoises survived their first winter – an appalling statistic.

The popularity of tortoises as pets nearly lead to their downfall.

In the mid-1970s Great Britain was still importing some 500,000 tortoises a year from Morocco, but increasing rarity and public concern in Europe lead Morocco to reduce its export numbers. British importers then turned their attentions to other countries such as Tunisia and the Balkans, bringing in other species of tortoises. By 1979 a voluntary quota of 100,000 animals was agreed by British importers but by 1984 the European Economic Community had imposed a ban on the import into the EEC of wild caught Hermann's, marginated and spur-thighed tortoises. Under the Convention for the international Trade in Endangered Species of Fauna and Flora (CITES) it became illegal to commercially trade in these species.

Many adults remember with fondness the tortoises they had or saw as children and wish to reacquaint themselves with these special creatures. Our knowledge of the needs of tortoises has increased greatly and the equipment to keep them happy and healthy is readily available at reasonable prices, but it is not cheap - nor should it be. There are no short cuts to success. Do your research, save your money, buy the correct set-up and invest in a healthy tortoise from a trustworthy source. Then enjoy the gift of a tortoise in your life.

Pictured:
An elderly tortoise –
probably in her sixties
and going strong!

Species & varieties

The most popular tortoises are the Mediterranean tortoises. Hermann's, marginated and spur-thighed tortoises are closely related. It is important to be able to accurately identify which type of tortoise (at least to the species level) that you have, as this can influence the care that they require. Amongst serious tortoise keepers and breeders there is also an increased emphasis placed on keeping single species groups as a means of reducing the risk of disease spread.

Hermann's Tortoise

Testudo hermanni

This is a true European tortoise – in fact a genus title of Eurotestudo has been suggested for these species, although this has not yet been accepted and will not be used in this book. The Hermann's tortoise is named after John Hermann, a naturalist from Strasbourg.

The most obvious features that distinguish this tortoise from other Testudo species are the lack of spurs on the thigh area (compare with Spur-thighed tortoises later) and the presence of a spur-like scale at the tip of the tail. In addition the shell is slightly flatter than those of the spur-thighed complex of tortoises. The presence of a divided supracaudal scute is a reasonably dependable (but not always present) identification (see subspecies descriptions). There is no hinge in the plastron.

There are considered to be two subspecies of Hermann's tortoises – the Western race T. hermanni hermanni and the Eastern race T. hermanni boettgeri, although there may be as many as four (if the Dalmatian Tortoise T. hermanni hercegovinensis and T. hermanni peleponnesica are confirmed as different species, rather than just geographic forms). In addition a dwarf Sardinia form T. hermanni sarda has been described from southern Sardinia. Amelanistic (light-coloured) T. h. hermanni have been recorded.

Pictured: Hermann's tortoise – note the subdivided supracaudal scale (the one immediately above the tail).

Western Hermann's Tortoise

T. hermanni hermanni

The Western Hermann's Tortoise is naturally found in southern France, southern Spain, Italy and the Balearic Islands. Of the two subspecies it is the smallest, with a carapace length rarely exceeding 165 mm in males and 190 mm in females.

The background colour of the shell is yellow with very dark to black markings on the scutes. The yellow colour can become particularly pronounced in captive-bred specimens that have little exposure to the outside. The last vertebral scute frequently has a well-defined, characteristic "keyhole" pattern. Virtually all of this subspecies have a divided supracaudal scute. On the underside, the plastral markings are obviously of two thick, black strips running the length of the plastron, divided by a bright yellow central line. The head is relatively smooth and elongated and is almost snake-like in appearance.

Eastern Hermann's Tortoise

NEAR THREATENED

T. hermanni boettgeri

This subspecies ranges across Serbia, Kosovo, Macedonia, Romania, Bulgaria, Albania, Greece and Turkey, with island populations on Corfu, Sicily and Sardinia.

T. h. hercegovinensis populates coasts of Bosnia and Herzegovina, Croatia and Montenegro. The mountainous areas of the Balkans, with separation of different populations, may in particular have produced a much greater geographic variation in appearance within this subspecies than in the Western form. Larger specimens of the eastern form readily exceed 200 mm carapace length, with females up to 300 mm. The background colour of the shell is a more greenish-yellow and the darker markings are not nearly so distinctly defined. Some 8 to 18% of Eastern Hermann's have an undivided supracaudal scute. The plastral markings are usually less distinct than those seen in the Western race and are more variable in appearance. The head is shorter and thicker than that of the Western race.

Pictured:
Hermann's tortoise is arguably one of the best tortoise species for our climate.

Sexing

Like all the Mediterranean tortoises, Hermann's tortoises cannot be sexed reliably until close to sexual maturity. The main differences between the sexes are listed in the table below.

FEATURE	MALE	FEMALE
ADULT SIZE	Smaller	Larger
TAIL	The tail is very much longer than in females and is much broader at the base. There is a longer cloacal slit in the underside of the tail.	The tail is relatively short and the cloaca less slit-like.
PLASTRON	In many male tortoises the plastron bows inwards to form a concavity.	The plastron is usually flat.
CARAPACE	Relatively flattened	Less flattened, more domed in appearance.

Male Testudo hermanni

(Hermann's tortoise)

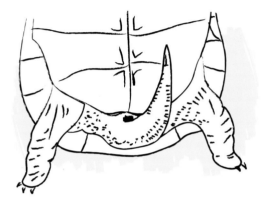

Note: Long pointed tail with horny pin at tip

Female Testudo hermanni

(Hermann's tortoise)

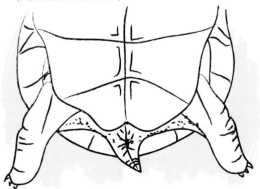

Note: Short pointed tail with small horny pin

Natural habitat

Hermann's tortoises inhabit relatively dry lands, typically hillsides and slopes with significant vegetation cover such as woodland and scrub that have access to sunnier, more open areas for basking and egg-laying.

In the eastern most part of its range, T. h. boetgerri lives alongside T. ibera, and is believed to occasionally hybridise with it. A dwarf Sardinia form T. hermanni sarda has been described from southern Sardinia. It lives alongside the dwarf form of the Marginated tortoise.

Suitability as a pet

Hermann's tortoises are suitable for vivaria and tortoise tables when small, but will need larger accommodation, ideally with access to the outdoors, as adults. Compared to some species they are relatively placid and females in particular are tolerant of each other's company. European in origin they are quite cold hardy and coupled with a tolerance of damp conditions this means that they are one of the best species for the climate of Great Britain.

Hermann's tortoises are listed by the IUCN as Near Threatened.

*Pictured:
Hermann's tortoises breed readily in captivity.*

Spur-thighed Tortoise
(Testudo graeca) Complex

The spur-thighed or 'Greek' tortoise (Testudo graeca) is a species with a wide geographic range that extends along the North African coast of the Mediterranean and into the Middle East. Such a wide homeland has lead to the evolution of many geographic races that are clearly distinguishable. The situation becomes even more complicated when some of these races are considered so different as to be categorised as different subspecies, or even species. As a result the whole population of spur-thighed tortoises is often referred to as a 'complex'.

As if that wasn't confusing enough, to further complicate matters tortoises of this complex have also been introduced into a variety of new areas including the Canary Islands, France, Sardinia, Italy, and Sicily. Whether these introductions are from known geographic areas or are of mixed origin is unknown. There is also some evidence of crossbreeding with native Testudo species such as T. hermanni in southern Spain.

Spur-thighed Tortoise

Originally the spur-thighed tortoise Testudo graeca was divided into four sub-species, namely Testudo graeca graeca, T. g. ibera, T. g. terrestris and T. g. zarudnyi. However re-assessment of the original species plus further detailed studies of tortoises collected and studied in the wild means that the spur-thighed 'complex' now includes the following species:

Testudo graeca graeca

Testudo graeca terrestris

Testudo (graeca) ibera

Testudo (graeca) zarudnyi

Testudo whitei

Furculachelys nabulensis

For added complexity it seems that the originally described spur-thighed tortoise Testudo graeca terrestris appears to be a dubiously defined species and may actually prove to one or more as yet poorly described species. It is also worth noting that the populations known as Libyan spur-thighed tortoises found in Cyrenacia in Libya (these were formerly considered a race of T. graeca) have now been renamed Testudo cyrenacia.

Confused? It's easy to be so. In the interests of consistency, the above nomenclature will be used (although it has by no means been agreed on by all authorities).

Spur-thighed or Greek Tortoise

Testudo graeca graeca

VULNERABLE

Yes, this tortoise does have spurs on its thighs, but no – it's not from Greece. In truth this tortoise is restricted to North Africa, primarily Libya, Tunisia and Morocco. Unfortunately many other tortoise species have in the past been erroneously described as this species, leaving the true T. g. graeca a difficult creature to categorise.

The spur-thighed tortoise is generally a small to medium sized tortoise. The background colour to the carapace is generally a yellowish to yellow-green colour with dark brown or black markings present on each of the carapacial scutes. Those markings that occur on the vertebral and costal scutes frequently take the form of a central, large spot. Further markings can be present around the outside of the scute that in some cases they form an almost ring-like appearance.

On the underside the plastron is hinged between the abdominal and femoral scutes. This is particularly obvious in adult females where this hinge allows an increase in the space at the hind end to facilitate egg-laying. The first vertebral scute is shield-like in appearance with rounded edges. The central marginal scutes have a fairly distinctive triangular marking. The supracaudal scute is single in the majority of individuals although a small percentage carry a divided supracaudal scute. Two spurs are visible either side of the tail – one on each thigh. It is these structures that give this tortoise its commonname, although the spurs rarely stick out beyond 2.5 mm.

Adult females are considerably larger than males (usually around 150 to 190 mm carapace length) and weigh around 1.0 to 1.5 kg. Males are usually no bigger than 180 mm and 1.0 kg in weight. In the wild, adult size is achieved at 25 to 35 years after which growth slows down but does not stop altogether.

Sexing

As for Hermann's tortoise.

Natural habitat

Typically found in dryer, almost arid environments with seasonal flushes of plants. In the northern part of their range this species hibernates during colder spells, whilst in the warmer southern areas it will aestivate over the hottest months.

Suitability as a pet

A good pet tortoise suitable for vivaria and tortoise tables when small, but requiring larger accommodation, ideally with access to the outdoors, as adults. Generally reasonably quiet with males not as aggressive as those of T. ibera. In households with both T. graeca and T. ibera, the graeca males can be seriously damaged by the aggressive activities of male ibera. This usually takes the form of serious shell damage by repeated ramming.

All spur-thighed tortoises are listed by the IUCN as Vulnerable.

Pictured:
In trouble? Except on very smooth surfaces, most tortoises can right themselves eventually.

Turkish Spur-thighed Tortoise

Testudo (graeca) ibera

T. graeca ibera is considered by some authorities to be a separate species - T. ibera - rather than a subspecies of T. graeca. Their natural range includes north-eastern Greece, Turkey, Iran, Iraq, Jordan and Syria, and going northward into Caucasus (Dagestan, Azerbaijan, Eastern Georgia and Armenia).

On initial inspection this subspecies resembles T. g. graeca, but a closer look reveals that the first frontal scute is angular, whereas that of T. g. graeca has curved edges. In older individuals the posterior marginals are often flared to some extent. The shell is often amber coloured, with the scutes having thick dark borders with a central spot on a yellowish centre.

Sexing

As for T. h. hermanni.

Natural habitat

Dry scrubby areas. Will hibernate during colder periods.

Suitability as a pet

Probably the most suitable of all the spur-thigh complex for life as a pet tortoise. Hatchlings and young are readily accommodated in vivaria and tortoise tables when small, but will need upgrading to larger accommodation, ideally with access to the outdoors, as adults. Turkish spur-thighed tortoises appear to tolerate the British climate very well, possibly because it occurs naturally in countries with environmental extremes. Males can be particularly aggressive towards other tortoises.

Spur-thighed Tortoise
Testudo graeca zarudnyi

This subspecies is a middle-eastern extension of the spur-thighed complex, being found in Iran and neighbouring Baluchistan (Pakistan), although it appears to be quite rare throughout its range. This is a relatively large tortoise with adult females readily weighing in excess of 3.5 kg and with a carapace length of over 280 mm. Males are smaller. The carapace is elongated in outline with the rear marginals upturned to give a flared appearance. It is an olive-brown colour with little obvious patterning.

The first (frontal) vertebral scute is often quite angular more like T. ibera than T. g. graeca. The fifth vertebral scute is not wider than the third in this tortoise. There are, however, noticeable diagonal reticulations on the vertebral and costal scutes. The marginal scutes at the front and back are often pointed with a translucent horny point to them. The plastron is dark with occasional lighter markings. The front legs are flattened and the covering scales are large and black – adaptations for burrowing. The skin of T. g. zarundyi is a pale olive-brown. Eyes are almond-shaped.

Sexing

As for T. h. hermanni.

Natural habitat

Dry, inhospitable landscapes often on rocky hillsides and plains. Typically found at an altitude of between 1,000 and 2,500 metres.

Suitability as a pet

As for the Turkish spur-thighed tortoise.

Another large tortoise that is occasionally encountered is Gilbert White's Tortoise Testudo whitei. This has a tortoise with a literary history - the famous naturalist Gilbert White wrote about his tortoise, Timothy, in his book Natural History and Antiquaries of Selbourne (1789). Timothy was collected in Algiers by a sailor around 1739-40 and bought by Gilbert's aunt. On her death in 1780 Gilbert inherited Timothy. The tortoise died in 1794, one year after White himself had passed on. The tortoise's shell was bequeathed to the Natural History Museum in 1853 and was subsequently identified as a distinct species – Testudo whitei. Gilbert White's Tortoise is found only in North Africa (Algeria) and is a large species with adult females on average reaching a carapace length of 240 to 280 mm and a weight between 2.0 to 3.5 kg. Males are smaller with a carapace length of up to around 250 mm and weights of around 2.0 to 2.5 kg. Care is as for spur-thighed tortoises.

Pictured:
Gilbert White's tortoise
is a large-growing
species.

Tunisian Tortoise
Testudo (Furculachelys) nabulensis

The Tunisian tortoise is a small tortoise - males have a carapace length up to 120 mm and are much smaller than females (130 mm +) with a much lower vaulted carapace. The heaviest females are likely to still be below 800 g. As its name suggests, this tortoise is found in Tunisia only.

In appearance these tortoises have a carapace with a yellowish background colour that bears black markings on the scutes. Both vertebral and costal scutes have a central black marking with the vertebral scutes also usually having a dark border along the leading and side edges. The costal scutes are coloured along the leading edge and variably on the other sides. The first costal in particular often lacks the leading border. The marginal scutes have a dark border along the leading edges - in some individuals these markings form triangular shapes. The plastron is not patterned other than having a large, poorly defined black marking in the central abdominal region. Two small thigh scales are present and these can be paired in some individuals.

Sexing

As for T. h. hermanni. In addition the supracaudal scute of males is curved inwards. In females this scute is reduced in size and does not curl inwards.

Natural habitat

Well vegetated grazing land or along the sunny, rocky verges of forests. Tunisian tortoises generally avoid dry sandy areas, although there are coastal populations.

Suitability as pets

These tortoises are relatively mild mannered although males will readily spar. Their small size allows them to be kept more easily in vivaria and they should not be subjected to hibernation except for relatively short, controlled spells if part of a breeding program. Tunisian tortoises, considered as part of the spur-thighed group, are listed by the IUCN as Vulnerable.

Marginated Tortoises
Testudo marginata

Along with Gilbert White's tortoise the marginated tortoise is considered to be the largest of the Mediterranean species with adult weight between 2.0 and 3.0 kgs. Females typically reach 220 to 280 mm carapacial length. Males can also have a length of up to 300 mm but some of this extra length is due to the caudal marginal flaring. The marginated tortoise also has the most limited range of southern Greece (from Mount Olympus southwards) with introduced populations in Sardinia and Tuscany.

Sexing

Males have an obvious narrower "waist" than females and the marginals are more flared. Otherwise as for T. h. hermanni.

Natural habitat

Dry scrubby or rocky areas, even in to coastal areas.

Suitability as a pet

Generally these are good tortoises to have as pets, but they are large and will eventually need access to a large amount of space. Outside, adults can do much damage to a well-maintained garden! Males however, can be very aggressive to other males and females during breeding.

Marginated tortoises are listed by the IUCN as Least Concern.

Pictured:
You can see the flaring of the caudal marginal scutes on this T. marginata.

Horsfield's or Russian Tortoise

Testudo (Agrionemys) horsfieldii

Horsfield's or Russian Tortoise
T. horsfieldii is sufficiently different from other Testudo species for it to have been placed by some authorities into its own genus of Agrionemys. This question has yet to be resolved, and so in the interests of simplicity I shall keep to the Testudo generic name in this book. There are thought to be at least three subspecies: T. horsfieldii kazachtanica, T. horsfieldii rustmovi and T. horsfieldii horsfieldii. The care of all three subspecies is similar. Horsfield's tortoise was named after the American naturalist Thomas Horsfield.

Horsfield's tortoise is largely an Asiatic species, naturally found in Eastern Iran, Afghanistan, Kazakhstan, Pakistan (including Baluchistan). Its range extends from as far west as the Caspian Sea to western China in the east.

Horsfield's tortoises are not large tortoises. They have a maximum size of up to 200 mm, but most are usually significantly smaller. From above, the outline of the shell is roughly circular, and this tortoise has a solid, stocky appearance. The colour of the carapace is a greenish-brown with poorly defined darker markings. It does share some features with Hermann's tortoise in that it has a spur-like scale on the tip of its tail (although this is not as prominent as with T. hermanni) and there is no hinge in the plastron. The skin on the legs, tail and neck is a brownish-yellow colour. One difference is that there are only four toes on each foot, distinguishing it from other Testudo species, which normally possess five toes on each of the front feet.

Sexing

Males have markedly longer tails. The plastron is usually flat in both sexes. Females are larger.

Natural habitat

As an inhabitant of the Russian steppes, this tortoise prefers open, grassy areas that are relatively dry. It is found on sandy steppes, rocky ground or on hillsides. They dig burrows up to two metres long with a widened chamber at the end; in Pakistan they take over the disused burrows of marmots. They can occur at high altitudes and have been discovered at heights of up to 2,300 m above sea level.

In many places throughout its range this tortoise is active for no more than 3 months of each year. Males will be above ground from early March to late May whilst females are found from mid March to mid June. This corresponds roughly to the period when their only food source, annual plants, is growing and available.

Suitability as a pet

Male Horsfield's tortoises can be quite aggressive and can inflict serious bites on other tortoises, although they do not "ram" quite so hard as other Testudo species. Conversely this means that females should not be mixed with males of other species as they can be seriously damaged by this violent activity. These tortoises are also excellent diggers and climbers.

Horsfield's are very cold hardy, but also require a dry environment; damp, humid environments increase the likelihood of respiratory disease. Finally, the long hibernation periods of some populations of this tortoise – which can be up to nine months of the year – means that these tortoises can be real eating machines. As a result, obesity can be problem.

Horsfields' tortoises are not covered by CITES legislation to the same extent as Hermann's and the spur-thighed group, so a great many are wild caught for the pet trade. As an example, at the time of writing (2010) CITES quotas permit Uzbekistan to export 22,000 wild-caught specimens, Tajikistan 20,000 wild-caught specimens and Kazakhstan 40,000 live specimens a year and Russia 18,000. There are now concerns that this tortoise is becoming scarce in certain parts of its range, causing the IUCN to list them as Vulnerable. Always make sure your Horsfield's tortoises are captive bred.

Aspects of tortoise biology & behaviour

The shell is what defines a tortoise. It surrounds and protects all of the internal organs and is an important reservoir of calcium. The upper shell is called the carapace and the underside the plastron. The joints between the carapace and plastron on either side of the body are the plastrocarapacial bridges.

The skeletal tortoise shell is composed of a number of bony plates, all fused together, and these are covered by a number of keratinised scutes. Although they overlie each other, the joints between these inner and outer two sets rarely overlap. This arrangement increases the overall strength of the shell.

In some species, such as the spur-thighed tortoise, the plastron is hinged at the junction of the hypoplastron and xiphiplastral plates, (which from the outside is between the abdominal and femoral scutes) forming a flap-like arrangement of the rear most section of the plastron. In the males of some species the plastron has a marked concavity affecting the abdominal scutes in particular. This is a secondary sexual characteristic and is not present in every male.

The skin

Tortoises have different types of skin on different parts of their body. Over the head, neck, upper forelimbs, tail and hind legs it has a thick leathery appearance with no obvious scaling. In these areas the skin is shed piecemeal and shedding is not synchronised like that in snakes. In contrast, the lower front legs are covered with large, tough scales that act as protective shields when the head and front legs are drawn in, effectively sealing off the front of the shell. They are also used for digging and can be very abrasive when rubbed across unwelcome hands!

Another skin type, most obvious on the shell are the scutes (Latin scutum: shield) or shields. In reality these are modified scales and usually there are 54 in total. The scutes are named according to their position. Like other scales elsewhere on the body, these have an outer layer of keratin (a substance very similar to our finger nails) which overlies a very thin skin layer, and this in turn covers the bone. The skin boundaries between the scutes are very thin and it is here that new keratin is produced. Unless worn away, this keratin is not shed like the rest of the skin, but is retained as characteristic rings. When tortoises are rapidly growing, these areas between the scutes often take on obvious yellowish white lined appearance.

The digestive system

Tortoises have no teeth. Instead they have a beak-like structure where both the upper and lower jaws carry thin blades of keratin that act as shears to slice through plant material. Any leaves that are too tough for the beak alone are torn apart. The tortoise first grips the food with its mouth, places a foot on it then tears it by pushing with its front feet and pulling back with the head. The large muscular tongue helps with this process as well. Food is therefore cropped and swallowed in large chunks without much chewing.

Most tortoise pets are largely plant-eaters (herbivores) but this diet can cause some problems. Much of the material that they eat is the structural plant compound cellulose. However, tortoises do not produce the enzymes necessary to digest this material and so they must rely upon bacteria present in the bowel to break down cellulose into compounds that the tortoise can utilise.

In the wild this bacterial degradation may be aided by other naturally present organisms. Wild Spur-thighed Tortoise Testudo graeca carry populations of the oxyurid pinworms Tachygometria spp. There are eight distinct species of these worms and amazingly they form an ecological community in the gut of T. graeca.

The different worm species are found in different parts of the large intestine. These worms are probably beneficial to the reptile in the wild state, churning food material in the large intestine as well as breaking it down into smaller particles to aid bacterial degradation. Unfortunately, routine worming will be likely to eliminate them from the tortoise gut. It may also be that inappropriate fibre levels tip the balance of these potentially beneficial organisms into pathogenic parasites.

The urinary system

Reptiles excrete their metabolic waste nitrogen as uric acid crystals – the white sand-like sludgy substance naturally present in their urine. Many owners mistakenly believe this to be calcium. A tortoise's bladder is a voluminous structure and can hold a significant volume of water. In the wild tortoises may have few opportunities to drink so the bladder acts as a water reservoir.

The reproductive system

Female tortoises have two ovaries. In a reproductively active female a bunch of egg-yolk like follicles form which are eventually released into the oviducts where they have a calcium-rich shell laid down around them.

Female tortoises have special crypts close to the end of their reproductive tract that can store sperm, possibly for several years.

Male tortoises have two testes that lie close to the kidneys. The phallus is an erectile organ present in the cloaca. It has a groove running down one side down which sperm is conducted during mating. When fully extended, the phallus is a large, almost mushroom-shaped structure that is usually darkly coloured. Some males routinely protrude the phallus and concerned owners regularly mistake this for an intestinal prolapse. The phallus plays no part in urination. Some female tortoises have a relatively large clitoris that can be easily mistaken for a phallus.

The cloaca

Tortoises, like other reptiles, do not have separate external orifices for the urine and genital tract and bowel – instead the gut, bladder and reproductive tract all communicate into a single chamber known as the cloaca. This is why tortoises often produce urine and faeces at the same time. The lining of the cloaca can absorb water. This is a useful trick because it means that a tortoise can sit in a puddle of water and take water on board without having to lower the head to drink – useful for keeping an eye out for predators.

Senses

Eyesight

Tortoise eyes are large, their vision is good and sight
is probably their main sense. Their colour vision is
also good as the retina is well supplied with colour
sensitive cones. It is thought that tortoises can
probably see in the ultraviolet spectrum.

Hearing

Tortoises have two ears that are set well back on the head. Each ear is covered by a large tympanic scale, which is the equivalent place to our eardrum.

Taste & smell

Tortoises have three ways of sensing food and other chemicals. These are:

- Olfaction (sense of smell) detected in the lining of the nose.

- Gustation (taste) detected on the surface of the tongue and mouth lining.

- Vomerolfaction. This picks up non-airborne scent particles from the tongue and lining of the mouth that are then transferred to the specialised vomeronasal organs situated in the roof of the mouth. Vomerolfaction may play a part in food detection and individual recognition based on an individual's scent profile. This may in part be how your tortoise recognises you!

Tortoises are 'sensitive' animals. Although they look like miniature bulldozers, the skin and shell are well supplied with nerve endings that are sensitive to touch, pain, heat, cold and other stimuli. As an example many female Hermann's tortoises will straighten their back legs and so raise their back end if the back half of the shell is gently scratched. This may be a reflex that would be triggered by pressure during normal mating.

Pictured:
A tough and hard
exterior masks an
animal sensitive to
its surroundings.

Behaviour

Tortoises, for a reptile, have a high IQ and can certainly learn to recognise their owner, just as their owner will learn that each tortoise is an individual with distinct likes, dislikes and behaviour patterns. In one study, tortoise hatchlings (Testudo graeca and T. hermanni) were shown not only to differentiate between colours but could also distinguish between different shaped objects.

Pictured:
Tortoises have a strong
muscular tongue.

Sociability

Many owners of single tortoises are concerned whether their tortoises are lonely or not. Tortoises are not social in the way that humans or dogs are. Keeping tortoises together will often encourage competitive feeding, but tortoises found consistently in the same part of a garden are likely to be there because it's the best place to be rather than for the company!

However, it is likely that tortoises do recognise and remember individuals that they encounter regularly and while most females will accept the presence of other females, the males of most species are intolerant of each other. Females can store sperm for quite long periods of time, which is thought to be an adaptation to a lifestyle where members of the opposite sex are only infrequently encountered.

Pictured:
Newly acquainted
tortoises will sniff each
other, nose to nose.

Although tortoises are often said to be territorial, it is probably more accurate to say that a tortoise will occupy a home range that is defended as occasion demands. This home range will include all that the tortoise needs to survive. The longer a tortoise remains in its home range, the better it will come to know its home and so utilise it more effectively.

The natural habitat of tortoises is a nutritionally poor and harsh environment with meagre resources that will not usually sustain large numbers of individuals. Population densities of around one individual per 150 square metres are not uncommon in the wild. It can be much lower depending upon the species and size of the individuals.

Male tortoises in particular are frequently territorial to a surprising degree, and will particularly target other males. Testudo ibera males can be especially aggressive and will cause serious damage to other, less aggressive species if housed together. Damage is commonly sustained to the shell of the subordinate, particularly at the back end of the carapace, with loss of part of the keratin scutes and exposure of the underlying bone. Bites around the head and legs can also be seen. Female tortoises will occasionally show similar behaviour, although it is rarely as intense as that seen in males.

Pictured: Sometimes male-female combinations work…and sometimes they don't.

Hatchlings & young tortoises

Tortoises behavioural characters vary greatly from individual to individual. However, it is generally the case that hatchlings and young tortoises are more timid than adults and can spend a great deal of time apparently hiding. This can be normal - a small tortoise would make a snack for a whole range of predators, so their behaviour at this vulnerable stage is not to attract attention.

Pictured:
A tiny tortoise takes a break before entering the world.

The importance of sunlight

Tortoises sunbathe, or more accurately, bask in sunshine both to warm up and regulate their body temperature (a process known as thermoregulation) and also to expose themselves to the beneficial ultraviolet rays from the sun.

Heat & thermoregulation

Tortoises are reptiles and are often inaccurately called 'cold-blooded'. This is because tortoises are unable to generate their own body heat like birds and mammals, so being able to regulate their body temperature is crucial. They do this by absorbing heat from external sources, such animals are termed ectotherms.

For a tortoise in the wild the main heat source is the sun and the tortoise warms up to the right temperature by basking. A tortoise can even fine-tune this process by altering the amount of time it spends in direct sunlight, changing the angle of its body to the sun to increase or decrease the surface area of shell exposed and by altering the blood flow to the shell and other skin surfaces. This latter method will affect how much of the heat absorbed is redistributed to the rest of the tortoise's body.

The temperature that the tortoise tries to achieve is called the Preferred Body Temperature (PBT), which for Mediterranean species of tortoises is around 30°C (86°F). The PBT is the temperature that the body of the tortoise works best at, including all of its internal chemical reactions, its digestion, immunity and its gut bacteria.

As their normal daily activity, most tortoises in the wild or in the garden will bask in the morning to warm up, and again during the late afternoon before seeking their place of rest for the night. During the midday period, when temperatures are highest, tortoises will seek shade.

The colour of the shell, especially that of the carapace, is also important. Black is the best absorber (and radiator) of heat.

Those tortoise species found in climatically cooler areas such as northerly populations of Hermann's tortoise, or at altitude such as Horsfield's tortoise, are darker than those from the more southerly countries.

Hibernation is a means of opting out of difficult times in nature. For some Mediterranean tortoises it helps them get through periods of adverse temperature and poor food availability.

Light

Tortoises are naturally found in parts of the world with high levels of sunlight and this is one of their most important environmental factors. From the point of view of the tortoise we can divide light into three different parts:

Photoperiod

The length of the day and night vary seasonally over the year. During the peak summer there can be over 14 hours of daylight, whilst during the middle of winter day length can be shortened to 10 to 12 hours. Tortoises monitor this with the pineal gland, and this helps to trigger the behavioural changes linked to preparation of hibernation as well as the hormonal cycles linked to breeding.

Spectrum

This refers to the wavelength, or colour, of light. Of particular importance is ultraviolet light, and this is divided into three parts – A, B and C.

- **Ultraviolet A** (UVA) has wavelengths of 320 – 400 nm (nanometres) and is important in triggering some normal behaviour patterns such as feeding. Tortoises can see into the ultraviolet spectrum and it may be that UVA affects how tortoises perceive their food and surroundings.

- **Ultraviolet B** (UVB) has wavelengths of 290 – 315 nm. This is the range of UV light that is needed for vitamin D3 synthesis by the skin. Vitamin D3 is required to absorb calcium out of the gut and into the body. Without it, calcium cannot be absorbed in significant quantities, even if large levels of calcium are present in the food. Vitamin D3 is produced in several stages. First of all, provitamin D is converted to a second compound – previtamin D – in the skin under the presence of UVB. Previtamin D is then further converted to vitamin D3 by a second reaction, but this is a temperature dependant change and so the tortoise must be at its preferred body temperature for this to happen.

Vitamin D3 is then further converted into more active substances in both the liver and kidneys. Vitamin D3 is probably needed for normal skin and immune function.

- **Ultraviolet C** (UVC) has even shorter wavelengths – around 250 – 260 nm, and is the most dangerous type, linked with skin cancers and sunburn. Tortoises are well protected from UVC with their highly pigmented skins.

Ultraviolet exposure in the wild is influenced by a number of variables including cloud cover, vegetation cover, time of day and so forth. It is, however, of crucial importance to the welfare of tortoises both in the wild and in captivity.

Intensity

Mid-summer sunshine at lower latitudes such as the Mediterranean is much more intense than that seen in more northerly countries such as Great Britain.

Moisture

The Testudo tortoises have evolved in semi-arid to arid environments, which have, at best, only seasonal rainfall. Many are found at relatively high altitudes, which again places them in low moisture environments. High humidity can predispose them to respiratory problems, a situation complicated by their unique anatomy that means that they cannot cough efficiently to eradicate any build up of phlegm or mucus from their windpipe and lungs.

Microclimates

In the dry world that these tortoises naturally live in, microclimates assume a great importance. These small, localised areas are where the surrounding geography and vegetation give rise to an environment significantly different to that of the more generalised landscape. With their smaller body size, hatchling and young tortoises will often seek out cooler and more humid microclimates – for example a disused rodent burrow may offer a more comfortable resting place in an otherwise baking landscape. In such burrows or under plants and rocks, these small and vulnerable creatures can hide from predators.

Predation

Tortoises occupy a similar ecological niche to small or medium-sized herbivores such as rabbits. Adult tortoises are taken by large raptors such as bearded vultures and golden eagles. Ground predators such as wild boar, rats and foxes also take their toll by plundering nests and hatchlings.

Longevity

Tortoises are naturally long-lived creatures. Well documented ages of 80, 90 or 100 years plus are not uncommon. One Mediterranean tortoise called Timothy was alleged to have hatched in Turkey around 1842 and died in 2004 at an estimated age of 160 years, having outlived six monarchs and two world wars. He turned out to be a she, but sex proved no barrier to a life in military service; Timothy was a mascot on British naval ship HMS Queen throughout the bombardment of Sebastopol in 1854 during the Crimean War. She later saw active service in both the East Indies and China that entitled Timothy to two service medals. In 1892 Timothy retired to Powderham Castle in Devon, home of the Earl of Devon.

A pet tortoise may live out your lifetime and that of your children too!

Acquiring a tortoise

Sources of tortoises

Before you buy your tortoise, read about them. Learn what you can of their care and requirements so that there are no surprises, financial or otherwise. Once you are happy that you can care for a tortoise in the way it should be, one of the most exciting parts of tortoise keeping awaits – purchasing your new companion.

There are several ways of obtaining a new tortoise, each of which has their own pros and cons.

Pet store

This is the most obvious source of a new pet tortoise, but there is a wide variation in the quality of tortoises and the service that you receive. Pointers towards a good shop are:

- The obvious health of the tortoises.

- The provision of correct housing. This should be reasonably clean and should include full spectrum lighting, obvious calcium supplementation on the food and no overcrowding or mixing of species.

- Plenty of ancillary equipment including lights, vivaria, substrate and nutritional supplements. Books and other helpful literature should also be available.

- Knowledgeable staff.

If all of the boxes above are ticked, its probably a good place from which to buy.

Internet

Purchasing a tortoise via the Internet might seem attractive, especially as the prices are often lower than high street pet shops. You are, however, buying these tortoises unseen – both the tortoise and their level of care – and there is a significant risk involved. Seriously ill tortoises have been sold to unsuspecting buyers by a small number of unscrupulous suppliers so beware. Run an Internet search on the company that you are considering buying from to see if there are any comments, good or bad, about them. Regulations govern the transport of all vertebrate animals so your tortoise should be shipped to you by an approved courier and not, as sometimes happens, via parcel post. Also, beware those companies that offer 'complete set-ups' without full-spectrum lighting. Such lighting is necessary and non-negotiable.

Private breeder

Buying from a private breeder should mean that you get an opportunity to assess the health of the tortoise as well as see its parents and the environment it was reared in. The quality of your tortoise will depend upon that of the breeder.

Tortoise welfare group

It may be that some tortoise welfare organisations have unwanted tortoises available for rehoming or sale. These will have been assessed by knowledgeable individuals and there will be significant backup in terms of expertise. Such rehomed tortoises do, however, usually remain the property of the organisation and there may be restrictions on certain activities such as breeding.

Private sale

A significant number of tortoises are bought from private homes or acquaintances. This is the least safe means of acquiring a new tortoise and in addition, some of these sales may be illegal, involving tortoises illegally brought into the country either by ignorant holidaymakers or animal traffickers. Remember that legally traded Annex A species of tortoises should have an Article 10 CITES certificate.

How to spot a healthy tortoise

Healthy tortoises, when awake, are usually bright, alert and can be quite responsive to what is going on around them. When walking, the body should be lifted right off the ground with the tortoise bearing its weight on the soles of all four feet – tortoises reluctant to move or that drag their back end should be avoided.

Check the plastron for signs of scuff-marks – these may indicate that the tortoise is unable to lift the weight of its body off the ground. Tortoises over the age of around twelve months old should have a solid shell.

Pictured:
Captive–bred tortoises are readily available today.

Very gently squeeze the shell – if the carapace or plastron is compressible then it may indicate metabolic bone disease (see Chapter Six), but do not use too much pressure as it can be painful and the shell can easily be damaged in small or calcium deficient tortoises. Significant doming of the scutes and markedly overgrown beaks and claws may also be symptoms of this condition.

The eyes should be bright, not sunken, with no obvious swelling of the eyelids or discharge. There should be no nasal discharge – a runny nose may indicate a serious infection. A healthy tortoise should have a good appetite if offered food.

Legislation

The main piece of legislation affecting tortoises worldwide is The Convention on the International Trade in Endangered Species of Flora and Fauna (CITES). CITES is designed to part control, and part monitor the trade of certain animals where there are certain concerns, for example if they are considered endangered. In the European Union species are listed as either Annex A or Annex B.

Annex A covers those species where only trade in captive bred animals is permitted and is tightly controlled. No specimens can be taken from the wild for commercial purposes.

Annex A Mediterranean (Testudo) tortoises are:

Testudo marginata

Testudo kleinmanni

Testudo hermanni

Testudo werneri

Testudo graeca

This list would include all subspecies, geographic races and those newer species such as Gilbert White's tortoise (T. whitei) and Testudo nabulensis that were previously covered under the T. graeca complex.

Annex B. This covers all other tortoises, including Horsfield's tortoise (T. horsfeldi).

CITES legislation means that in the UK the sale of those tortoises listed under Annex A requires certification from the Department of the Environment, Food and Rural Affairs (DEFRA). The certificate that is required is an Article 10.

An Article 10 certificate can be one of the following:

1. **A Specific Specimen Certificate.** This is issued for a tortoise that is permanently identified. In practice this means that it has been microchipped. Individual discernable/visible characteristics will not suffice. This certificate accompanies an individual tortoise throughout its life and should be passed on to the new owner if the tortoise is sold.

The microchip number will be listed on the certificate and the address need not be updated if the tortoise changes hands (see next).

2. **A Transaction Certificate.** This will be issued if the tortoise is too small to be microchipped (or if it is a very rare specimen). This certificate covers one transaction only. If the tortoise is to be resold then a new Transaction Certificate needs to be obtained. As of August 2009 the address at which such a tortoise is kept must be on the Article 10 that accompanies that tortoise. This means that DEFRA must be informed of a change of ownership or address and a new Article 10 subsequently re-issued. A charge is levied by DEFRA for this service. Note that this requirement is also true for pet shops, which are now obliged to change their Article 10 information to comply on purchasing Annex A species, which must then again be updated at the time of sale. It is an offence not to do so i.e to sell an Annex A species with an address on the Transaction Certificate that is different from that of the vendor.

Other points to be noted:

1. The sale of Annex B species does not require such certification. For our purposes this only applies to Horsfield's tortoise.

2. Giving away an Annex A species, for example as a gift or to a tortoise charity, does not require an Article 10. However, I would always strongly recommend that with each transfer of a tortoise a letter handing over ownership to the new owner should be obtained.

3. Annex A species also require Article 10 certificates if:
   1. They are to be used as breeders. It is illegal to sell captive-bred young from non-certificated adults.
   2. They are on public display e.g. as part of a zoological collection.

It is important to realise that the sale of an Annex A tortoise without appropriate certification is illegal in the UK. For further guidance please look at www.ukcites.gov.uk and seek out the section on Guidance Notes for Tortoise Traders.

For countries other than the UK please seek advice from the local authorities so that you comply with any legislation.

Aside from the above, in the UK there is no legislation governing the actual keeping of Mediterranean tortoises as pets, other than the welfare considerations under the Animal Welfare Act 2006. This is not true for other countries however.

In the USA there may be both state and federal laws governing whether you can keep pet reptiles, including Mediterranean tortoises. If in doubt then a good place to start is the United States Fish and Wildlife Service.

For those interested in keeping Mediterranean tortoises in Australia, please consult the Department of Sustainability, Environment, Water, Population and Communities. At the time of writing it would appear that the keeping of non-native reptiles is severely restricted and if allowed at all, permits will be required.

Microchipping

This is considered the best way of permanently identifying a tortoise, both to comply with legislation and to increase the chance of you getting your tortoise back in the event of it straying or being stolen. It involves the insertion of a microchip transponder into the tortoise and in the UK the recommended site is in the left thigh. At present it can only be legally performed by a veterinary surgeon as the hole left in the relatively inelastic tortoise skin does require closure – either by suture or tissue glue. Tortoises with a carapace length of less than 10 cm are considered too small for microchipping.

Plastron photocopying

Another way of identifying your tortoise is to regularly photograph or photocopy the plastron. Each tortoise has unique markings on its' plastron and can be identified by these. This means of identifying individuals is not adequate for CITES purposes.

Housing

In Chapter Three we looked at some aspects of a tortoise's natural history and how important such parameters like temperature and sunlight are. These vital needs must be addressed – a tortoise will not 'adapt' to a life without them, instead it will eventually become ill and die.

How complex or simple the housing necessary for the correct keeping of these Mediterranean tortoises depends very much upon the species and life-stage of the tortoises that one is keeping. The simplest way to keep hardy tortoises such as Hermann's tortoise and Turkish spur-thigh is free range in a walled garden or in a large, naturalised pen. More delicate species will need vivaria or 'tortoise tables' for them to thrive long-term. This will also apply to hatchling and youngsters of the other species as well.

However, each method of care is not exclusive to the others and can be mixed, for instance, keeping the more delicate species in runs outside in the summer often works to their benefit, whilst sick adults of the hardier species can be wintered in vivaria.

Here are some general recommendations on keeping groups of tortoises together:

- Never mix species. This is for both behavioural and veterinary reasons.

- Wherever possible only keep one male to a pen.

- Females can, in general, be kept in groups without too much aggression.

- In mixed sex groups, a minimum ratio of 1:2 males to females is recommended.

Vivaria

Vivaria are enclosed, often rectangular indoor housings that come in a variety of different materials and styles. Dedicated reptile vivaria should be used for captive tortoises. They are made from many different substances including wood, MDF, plastics and glass that can either be bought ready made, as flat packs or even built from scratch. The potential size and scope of a vivarium is limited only by the available space and the depth of your wallet. Key features of a good vivarium are:

- Access via lockable sliding doors at the front of the vivarium. This greatly simplifies routine maintenance.

- Water proofing. Tipped water containers and urine can lead to rotting wood unless the joints are silicone sealed.

- Ventilation - this is normally ventilation is achieved by installing grids of mesh or plastic at opposite ends of the vivarium. Normally these grids are positioned at different heights so that as warm air rises it exits from the higher ventilation panel whilst fresh air is drawn in from the lower.

- With glass vivaria opaque strips may need to be placed along the bottom of the sides to provide a visual barrier that the tortoise can perceive.

- Perhaps the most difficult aspect of keeping tortoises (and other reptiles) in vivaria is how to recreate the sun in the box to provides both light and heat. Modern reptile accessories make this a great deal easier than it used to be, but it is still more convenient to separate lighting from heating and this is reflected in the commercially available products. This separation of these two key elements allows independent control where necessary.

Pictured:
A variety of lights are
available for use in
vivaria.

Heat

In its simplest form this can be provided by a spotlight or other tungsten bulb that acts as a radiant heat source.

This will encourage your tortoise to bask beneath it as it thermoregulates. Ideally the bulb should be placed to one end of the vivarium so that a temperature gradient forms along the length of the vivarium to allow the tortoise to select the temperature it prefers. These lights should be connected to a thermostat so that the vivarium does not overheat, and to a timer so that the light is not on for 24 hours a day (or worse still is perpetually flicking on and off as the thermostat reacts to the temperature). To solve this second potential problem, there are ceramic bulbs available that only give out radiant heat and these are to be recommended because such bulbs can provide heat throughout the day and night irrespective of the lighting regime. A less satisfactory alternative are red bulbs which produce heat and only visible red light, which is less disturbing to the tortoises at night. Note that tortoises can see the colour red.

Pictured:
Large tortoise such as one opposite, need spacious accommodation with suitable heating and lighting.

There are also some blue bulbs available that emit light in the UVA spectrum.

Heat mats are also readily available and these can be placed either under the vivarium or on the side to provide localised warm areas; they are, however, insufficient to warm a whole vivarium and should be considered as supplementary heating only. The temperature beneath the basking light should be around 35°C (95°F) with a background temperature of around 20 to 25°C (68 to 77°F). A nighttime fall to 15°C (59°F) is easily tolerated, even by hatchlings.

Lighting

Sunlight coming through your window from outside is not sufficient for the needs of tortoises, because glass filters out any UV lighting. We have to provide this artificially and typically it is provided by fluorescent tubing that has been tweaked to produce the important wavelengths of light for tortoises, as well as produce a light that renders more natural colouring and so appears like normal sunlight. These fluorescent tubes available to herpetologists emit light in the most important parts of the spectrum including UVB and UVA. There are some important points to remember with this kind of lighting:

- Light intensity falls off inversely with distance from the light source so that if one doubles the distance between the tortoise and the light tube, the intensity of the light is halved. Therefore suspending a full spectrum light several feet above a tortoise will be of little use. The ideal distance will usually supplied by the manufacturer, but if in doubt suspend the tube around 30 to 45 cm above the top of the carapace.

- Many lights are rated according to their UVB output, and this is indicated by a figure at the end of the trade name. Typically these ratings are 2.0, 5.0, 8.0 and 10.0. Each figure refers to the percentage output of UVB and so a light rated as 5.0 should produce around 5% of its output as UVB. Mediterranean tortoises should have lights rated as 5.0 or 8.0.

- The shape of the tube affects the area of exposure to suitable levels of ultraviolet light. The compact tubes (which resemble economy light bulbs in appearance) produce a fairly narrow beam of ultraviolet light whilst the longer cylindrical fluorescent tubes emit a more even beam over the length of the tube. This could be important for larger tortoises, as they may only be able to expose a small area of their shell or skin to ideal UV light levels if only the compact bulbs are used.

Ideally the tubes should extend the full length of the vivarium, but if not, situate them close to the heat source so that the tortoise will be exposed to the beneficial lighting as it basks.

- Mesh tops can filter out up to 50% of the UV-B radiation.

- The lighting is best connected to a timer so that the tortoise has a regular day/night pattern, at around 14 hours day to 10 hours night. This also gives us the ability to manipulate the lighting regime to help with preparation for breeding or hibernation if required.

- Always buy those lights specifically designed for reptiles, as many fluorescents said to mimic the sun are colour rendered to deceive our eyes and do not emit the correct spectrum. Unsuitable lights include those made for aquaria, general fluorescents available from hardware stores and ultraviolet tubes marketed for inclusion in pond filters. The latter are especially dangerous as they emit UV-C and can cause serious eye damage. Glass filters out UV light and so the correct tubes are made from quartz – which makes them more expensive than ordinary fluorescents. Price can therefore be a rough guide to your purchase.

- Unfortunately the UV output declines over time and so these tubes need replacing every eight to twelve months. Failure to change is a common cause of metabolic bone disease in tortoises kept in vivaria. In the past few years lighting that emits both the correct spectrum and heat have become available and work well. Combining the two better mimics natural sunlight, but it does take away some of the flexibility in having both functions separate. Always provide your tortoise with a hide of some sort so that it can retreat from the light should it want to.

Pictured:
The correct environment is essential for hatchling tortoises.

Hygiene

Cleanliness becomes a serious issue within vivaria. It is very tempting to try to set up naturalistic landscapes in vivaria, but tortoises, especially larger ones, are inadvertently destructive creatures that will rapidly bulldoze through any habitat arrangements.

Naturalistic vivaria are harder to keep clean because urine soaks readily into the substrate and faeces can be missed; there may even be a disincentive to remove soiled material in case it spoils the appearance. It is generally better to keep to a basic setup using newspaper as a substrate. This is cheap and cheerful and can be easily removed if soiled. There are some products specifically marketed as tortoise beddings and these include pellets based variously upon straw, hay or hemp. These are usually fine provided that spot-cleaning is done regularly. The advantage to these substrates is that accidental ingestion is unlikely to cause any problems.

Avoid bark chippings and other wood-based substrates as these can be accidentally eaten and act as potential intestinal foreign bodies. They also harbour moisture, increasing the risk of bacterial and fungal diseases.

Tortoise tables

This popular way of keeping tortoises indoors is based on a table structure where the tabletop is surrounded by a lip or wall of sufficient height to stop the tortoise from climbing out. Heating and lighting is as described under Vivaria, but is suspended over the table. With this housing the surface area available for the tortoises is much larger than is generally the case with vivaria.

Further benefits are that ventilation is excellent and it also raises the tortoises up to a level that allows you to interact with them more easily. Just make sure that there is no way that the tortoise can scale the walls! Several commercial models are now available, at least one of which has a mesh top that can be fastened down to protect your tortoises and has a metal bar as part of the frame that crosses over the table from which lights and heaters can be suspended.

Greenhouses & outdoor buildings

Greenhouses, conservatories and similar have the advantage of space and, with the correct choice of materials, exposure to natural heat and sunshine. Temperature is often higher inside a greenhouse than out, but this can fluctuate markedly depending upon levels of sunshine. Shading of some description may be needed to iron out temperature instabilities (although this will inevitably reduce exposure to sunlight), or as an alternative install automatic greenhouse vents that open and close as the temperature rises or falls.

To complete the set-up, installing thermostatically controlled heat lamps and full spectrum lighting over the floor or individual pens will allow you to increase the hours of 'daylight' during the winter if necessary.

Pictured:
Mediterranean
tortoises do best
outside in the sun.

The garden

Large individuals of the hardier species including Testudo hermanni, T. ibera, T. marginata and T. whitei can, and arguably should, be kept outdoors from the spring into late autumn. If the garden is not escape proof then large pens will be needed to provide the necessary amount of natural grazing. Pens can also be utilised as summer accommodation for more delicate species.

I would recommend pens for Horsfield's tortoises too, because although this species is very cold hardy it has an uncanny knack of becoming invisible in a garden setting. It is also a seasoned escapologist able to climb and dig its way out many gardens. In a pen, you know your tortoise is in there somewhere...

There are several advantages to keeping tortoises outdoors:

- Space. Many of these tortoises are medium to large in size and simply require a lot of space to move around.

- Natural grazing. A more natural diet is easily provided by keeping tortoises on 'lawns' of grass and clover and allowing them access to wild plants such as dandelions.

- Access to unfiltered sunlight.

- Exposure to natural seasonal changes. This includes seasonal variations in day length that initiate pre-hibernation behaviour.

For every good point, there is a bad point however:

- Potential predators. Rats, foxes, magpies and even pet dogs can predate, or at least badly injure, tortoises at liberty in the garden.

- Exposure to 'natural' hazards such as garden ponds (which should, wherever possible, be fenced off), lawnmowers, herbicides and overzealous gardeners. Some garden plants may be toxic such as daffodils and foxgloves (Digitalis sp).

- Parasite build up. Gardens can become contaminated with roundworm eggs that can overwinter and re-infest the tortoise the following spring. This is especially so if the winter is mild.

- Variable weather. In Great Britain and other northern latitude countries periods of good summer weather can be regularly interspersed with bouts of cold and often very wet weather. At such times those tortoises outside appear to virtually 'shut down' - they stop feeding and moving around, waiting patiently for the weather to improve.

- Escape.

- Theft.

However it is certainly true that the benefits of time spent outside outweigh any potential problems.

When building a tortoise enclosure or adapting a pre-existing garden into an area suitable for tortoises the first consideration is access to sunshine, as this is about the only environmental factor that we cannot easily change or substitute. Ideally, the garden should be south-facing with full sun falling on to some part of it throughout the day (or at least on those days when it is sunny). This will allow the tortoises to thermoregulate naturally and effectively, and they will soon learn the best places to bask at a given time of day. Providing or creating south-facing slopes will also help them to do this.

Keeping tortoises loose in your garden involves either penning the tortoises away from the garden (and your flowerbeds) or fencing the garden off from your tortoises using low walls or raised beds. There are obviously a number of ways that one can construct a tortoise pen or tortoise-proof garden.

Walls can be constructed from a variety of materials ranging from brick and stonework through to railway sleepers, or even just wooden boards or fencing. Whatever material is used it should be solid so that the tortoises cannot see out, and the top edge should be at least 45 cm above the ground, preferably with a slight inward overhang. The barrier should also extend some 30 cm below the ground level as well, to reduce the risk of escape by burrowing. Garden gates can be made tortoise-proof by having lift-out boards across the gap that can be stepped over or removed as required.

Free-standing water in a shallow dish should always be available. You may never see your tortoise drink, but it does not mean that it never does.

Basic management of tortoise enclosures involves the regular removal of faeces as soon as seen, as this will help to reduce the risk of parasite build up (tortoise faeces make an excellent addition to the compost heap). Make sure that you remove any uneaten food daily, as this may help to attract rats and other opportunist rodents, and weed out any potentially dangerous plants.

A tortoise kitchen

Water

Tortoises, like all animals, need water to survive, but the habitats where tortoises live are relatively dry environments, so what is a thirsty tortoise to do? A standing water source may be quite a distance away and a tortoise cannot cover long distances like a large mammal can nor can it fly over natural obstacles like a bird to reach a water source.

Tortoises have solved this problem by a combination of behavioural and internal means. Together these adaptations mean that Mediterranean tortoises are good at collecting water and keeping it for as long as possible. Make no mistake about it, if a thirsty tortoise finds a river, a stream (or a puddle of water after a rainstorm), it will drink, and pet tortoises should always have access to water.

If a tortoise is able to feed early in the day it may access dew-covered vegetation as a bonus. In addition, many of the natural chemical reactions that occur inside the body generate molecules of water that can be a significant percentage of the tortoise's total water needs.

Water painstakingly harvested by the body needs to be stored and the best place for this is the urinary bladder. When full, it can occupy up to 40% of the volume inside the shell. If the tortoise is in danger of becoming dehydrated it can absorb water directly across the wall of the bladder and back into its body – something that mammals like us are unable to do.

Diet & feeding

There is a considerable amount of incorrect information and recommendations on the feeding of pet tortoises.. A tortoise has a different digestive system from us, and I have known many tortoises with food addictions, for example to banana or peas. These addictions are often encouraged by owners who just want to see their tortoise eat, irrespective of what it is they are eating.

So lets look at the basics – what these tortoises need and what they would consume in the wild.

Testudo tortoises are herbivores and obtain approximately 55 to 75% of their energy needs from carbohydrates (especially sugars), with less from protein (15 to 35%) and even less (below 10%) from fats. Studies on the wild Spur-thighed tortoise (T. graeca) found that its diet consists mostly of the Plantain family Plantago (30%), the Daisy family Compositae (26%)and Bedstraw family Rubiaceae (10%) whilst for Hermann's tortoise (T hermanni) the diet largely constituted consisted of Bedstraw family (25%), Peaflower family Leguminosae (22%), Daisy family (10%) and Buttercup family Ranunculaceae (8%).

Two interesting facts that came from these studies was that the wild diet had a typical protein content of 2.75% and an average calcium to phosphorus ratio of 3.5:1.

The next piece of the tortoise dietary jigsaw is the nutritional content of food. Food consists of a variety of different nutritional elements that add up to the quality of any given food. Good quality food provides what the tortoise requires whilst poor quality food is either deficient in some or all of these aspects, or else is inappropriate for the needs of the tortoise.

The main considerations are:

Water

Water clean, free-standing water should always be available.

Protein

Protein is needed for growth and repair of the body. Testudo tortoises have evolved to thrive on a low protein diet, but by feeding standard "supermarket" foods it is very easy to overdo this, triggering gut disorders and problems with excessive growth.

Fat

Fat is utilised relatively poorly by Testudo tortoises, but some dietary fat is essential. Reproductively active females need some dietary fat because most of the egg yolk consists of fatty materials. Too high a fat diet can result in liver disease (hepatic lipidosis).

Carbohydrates are the main energy source for terrestrial chelonia. These carbohydrates are simple sugars and starches produced by plants during photosynthesis and are absorbed in the small intestine. Excessive carbohydrate intake can not only lead to gut upsets, but also hepatic lipidosis as excess is converted into fat and stored in the liver.

Fibre

Fibre is important in two main ways. First of all part of it is digested by gut bacteria, which break it down to smaller molecules that can be absorbed and used by the tortoise for energy. Secondly, its presence promotes normal gut motility and stool formation, both of which are vital to a normal gut environment.

Vitamins

Tortoises require a number of vitamins to remain healthy.

Minerals

The mineral content of food plants is largely a reflection of the underlying geology. For Testudo tortoises the most important mineral in the diet is calcium, especially because many of the foods offered to tortoises are low in this substance. As we have seen it is needed in large quantities compared to other minerals.

Considering that the parts of the plant that are usually eaten are the leaves and flowers, we can come up with a simple blue-print for the type of food that Testudo tortoises ought to be given. In principle the bulk of the diet should be high in fibre, high in calcium and low in protein.

Fibre is important to the normal functioning of the bowel and fibre levels as high as 30 to 40% may be necessary to ensure normal growth rates. Offering green and leafy foods as the bulk of the diet is a good way of ensuring plenty of fibre. Ideal foods would include dandelion leaves (and flowers), grasses, sow thistle, clover and watercress. Include also various lettuces as part of the food intake. Lettuce leaves are a good source of water and are usually so palatable to the tortoise that they will accept it even when coated with vitamin and mineral supplements. Remember that like all foods, lettuce in itself is not nutritionally complete, so a diet of only lettuce will cause problems.

Tortoises, because of their bony shell, have a high need for calcium in their food. A study into wild North American gopher tortoises (Gopherus agassizi) has demonstrated that they will selectively seek out and eat those plants with naturally high calcium levels and it is highly probable that Testudo species do so as well.

The availability of calcium in the food of the tortoise is governed by a number of different factors, one of which is the level of phosphorus present.

Protein levels should be kept low. Testudo tortoises are almost exclusively vegetarian, but because their wild-diet is so nutritionally poor they will on occasion supplement it with other foods. For example, if they come across the carcass of a bird or similar, they may eat it as a means of increasing their protein intake. This is a survival instinct that allows tortoises in the wild to maximise their use of the environment, but this is different from regularly feeding them on dog or cat food, a practice that can cause problems long-term. The high protein levels of these foods make them tasty to the tortoise, but the urge to feed them on these should be resisted.

Specific food recommendations should be regarded as guidelines only. Too prescriptive a list would risk offering a narrow dietary range, yet some guidance is regularly sought. The key to providing a good diet is to offer variety with calcium supplementation. A recommended range would include, but is not restricted to:

Dandelion (Taraxacum)

Hawkbits (Leontodon)

Hawkweeds (Pictis)

Sowthistles (Sonchus)

Chickweed (Stelaria)

Plantains (Plantago spp.)

Cat's ears (Hypochoeris,)

Honeysuckle (Lonicera)

Hawkbeards (Crepis)

Vetches (Vicina)

Trefoils (Lotus)

Red and white clovers (Trifolium)

Mallows (Malva)

Bindweeds (Calystegia)

Sedums (Sedum)

Ivy-leaved Toadflax (Cymbalaria muralis)

Robinia

Acanthus

White and Red Dead Nettles (Lamuim)

Hedge mustard (Sisymbrium)

Bramble (Rubus fruticosus)

Nasturtiums (Tropaeoloum)

Lettuce (not Iceburgh)

Rocket (Diplotaxus)

Watercress (Nasturtium)

Carrot tops (Daucus)

Mustard cress (Lepidum and Brassica (Sinapsis))

Brassicas e.g. cabbage, cauliflower, Brussel sprouts (in moderation only).

Buttercups (Ranunculaceae)

A potentially toxic plant, but nevertheless often eaten readily and with no ill effects by Testudo species. Note that these flowers form part of the natural diet of both wild T. Hermanni and T. horsfieldi. Offer only with care.

Leafy greens selected from the list above should be the mainstay for their diet. Water cress and dandelion leaves are especially valuable because they are naturally high in calcium, although not enough to supply the total needs for a tortoise.

Some greens should only be given in moderation. Members of the cabbage family such as cauliflowers, brussel sprouts and broccoli should be offered as no more than 10% of the total diet, because they contain substances called goitrogens. These goitrogens antagonise thyroxine and so can induce low thyroxine levels (hypothyroidism). Spinach, rhubarb leaves and daffodils contain oxalic acid, which can be an irritant to the gut lining or can trigger bladder stone formation, as well as binding calcium into a form that is unavailable to the tortoise.

Other foods

Flowers, including dandelions and nasturtiums are readily taken. Be careful when offering flowers because some may be dangerous. Deaths have been recorded from feeding just a few daffodil flowers (see Toxic Plant List).

Vegetables are also useful additions to leafy greens. For example, cucumbers and courgettes are valuable sources of water. Red and yellow vegetables such as peppers and grated carrots can be offered. If eaten, they provide a good source of vitamin A. Tomatoes are frequently offered and although they too are a good source of water, nutritionally they are acceptable only as a small percentage of the tortoise's diet.

Beans and peas are relatively high in protein and are often readily taken, but in some cases this can be to the exclusion of other foods. The protein content can be too high in these foods, and they also contain phytic acid that, like oxalic acid, will bind calcium into a form unavailable to the tortoise.

In the case of fruits the dietary profile is in general inappropriate for these animals. As a rough guide do not offer fruit to spur-thighed or Horsfield's tortoises as they are less able to cope with high carbohydrate levels; otherwise feed no more than 10% fruit.

Meat should not be given in any form, especially tinned dog or cat food. It is often said that tortoises will take snails. Hermann's tortoises in particular seem to enjoy them, whilst most spur-thighed tortoises will usually ignore these garden pests.

Dietary supplements

The undoubted high requirement for calcium by tortoises means that if in doubt it is better to be cautious and provide a vitamin/mineral supplement. This is especially true of hatchling and young tortoises with a lot of growing to do and if indoors, no access to soils or other natural mineral sources.

Calcium is best supplied in a commercial calcium supplement (there are many available) or as cuttlefish, Many of these are combined with multivitamin complexes. If you opt for these do make sure that it is a supplement designed with reptiles in mind and so has vitamin D3, not vitamin D2. If there is good provision of ultraviolet light, either from natural sunlight or from full spectrum lighting, then calcium carbonate powder, or even limestone, can be given. Wherever possible make sure that the calcium supplement is phosphorus free. Eggshells, which consist largely of calcium carbonate, do need sterilising first to reduce the risk of Salmonella infections.

Pelleted foods

As tortoises have increased in popularity more pet food companies have developed and marketed suitable pellets for tortoise. Some of these are very good if used correctly, although some of the more generalised ones are far too high in protein and low in fibre for herbivorous species. They are, however, usually very palatable and can form a good basis for a tortoise's diet as they contain good levels of calcium and vitamins.

Tortoises are grazers who tend to crop a few choice pieces and then move on. Rarely will they stay in one place and graze a plant until it is level with the ground. Such behaviour means that if a tortoise is presented with a pile of food, it will eat some, but may then walk through the remaining food, possibly spoiling it further by defaecating or urinating on it. This may appear wasteful and frustrating for the tortoise owner, but is perfectly normal. Therefore try to offer food in relatively small amounts twice daily. This reduces waste and mimics a more natural feeding pattern.

For tortoises kept at large in the garden that have access to lawns and herbaceous borders, only a minimum of dietary supplementation is often needed. This free-range lifestyle closely resembles a more wild-type situation. A sign of a healthy diet is if the droppings are well formed, dark and fibrous. Runny faeces, considered by many to be normal, are often the result of too low a fibre intake, although it can be a sign of parasitism.

Pictured: Several types of pelleted foods are available – feed only as part of diet.

Diet related diseases

Diseases and problems related to improper diet are quite common in tortoises.

Loss of appetite

Tortoises can go off their food for a variety of reasons and so a loss of appetite should not be considered a disease, but just an indicator that something may be developing. In the autumn a reducing food intake may just indicate preparedness for hibernation, but in the middle of summer it could be something more sinister. Tortoises not kept at their preferred body temperature may simply not eat so that during periods of cooler weather, outdoor tortoises may literally 'shut down' until warmer weather returns. This is normal and should not be a cause of concern.

Loose droppings

This is common in tortoises fed on a diet high in fruit and low in fibre. The high levels of soluble sugars and starch are not digested by the tortoise, and instead ferment in the large bowel causing diarrhoea.

Metabolic bone disease (mbd) & excessive protein intake

These can be very similar in presentation and, because they are due to poor diet, affected tortoises can show signs of both conditions simultaneously. The skeleton can be badly affected and any limb swelling, fracture or paralysis should be considered as a possible sign of an underlying MBD or similar. Metabolic Bone Disease is actually a group of skeletal disorders that are largely – but not exclusively - dietary related. Common causes include a dietary calcium deficiency, a dietary calcium/phosphorus imbalance, a dietary vitamin D3 deficiency, lack of exposure to ultra violet light, dietary protein deficiency or excess and liver, kidney or intestinal disease.

Typically they are seen in young, rapidly growing tortoises, fed on a diet where the protein levels of their diet is too high relative to its calcium levels. Bones have both a protein and mineral component, and so are doubly affected on such diets.

The bones of the shell are not mineralised (hardened) properly making them weak and easily deformed; the leg bones become over long but are weak and tend to bend and deform under the weight of the tortoise.

Affected tortoises often show the following deformities:

- The scutes of the shell are visibly mounded in appearance as excessive keratin is produced. These scutes also have a "plastic" like appearance, quite unlike that of normal, healthy tortoises.

- The shell is palpably soft. The skeleton is a reservoir of calcium, and calcium is being continually drawn out of the bone and into the blood stream to be used for normal physiological activities. Only once 60 to 70% of the calcium has been withdrawn from the shell will it be weak enough to compress. By the time this can be felt, the tortoise is already in severe difficulties. Affected tortoises have shells that can be easily compressed (remember if you do this it is painful to the tortoise). The carapace will often slope from front to back, because the front part is supported by the regular withdrawal of the head and neck.

- Some affected tortoises are physically unable to lift themselves up, because the long bones of the limbs, as well as the joints themselves are deformed. A healthy tortoise will lift the full weight of its body on to its soles.

- The beaks and claws of these tortoises are often grossly overgrown – partly because too much keratin is produced and partly because these reptiles are often on too soft a diet for adequate wear.

- Tortoises with extremely low blood calcium levels may go very floppy. This is because all muscles (including the heart muscle) need calcium to function correctly. Tortoises this badly affected carry a very poor prognosis.

Should a tortoise start to manifest these signs then one should immediately consider the following:

Diet

Reassess the possible protein, fibre and mineral content of the diet. Consider increasing or improving the calcium content of the diet. Remember, that by around one year of age the carapace and plastron should be solid in a healthy tortoise. Also, in the wild, young tortoises will take up to ten years to reach a carapace length of 10 cm. In captivity I have seen captive-bred tortoises fed on high protein/low calcium diets reaching adult size at eighteen months old, accompanied by gross skeletal deformities. Always aim for a slower growth rate by selecting a more appropriate diet.

Lighting

Make sure there is provision for ultraviolet lighting. If fluorescent tubes are used check that their positioning is appropriate (usually around 30 cm above the animal), close to a heat source (to encourage basking) and that they are changed regularly (every eight to twelve months). Supplementing with dietary or injectable vitamin D3 may be worth considering, but overdose can occasionally occur.

Temperature

Encourage a temperature drop at night if the tortoise seems otherwise well.

Lethargy/ Anorexia (loss of appetite)

If the tortoise shows severe signs or is lethargic or anorexic then seek veterinary advice, as secondary infections are common in such animals. Your tortoise may need radiographs, blood tests or other tests to establish what is causing the problem.

References

Highfield A.C. 2000 The Tortoise and Turtle Feeding Manual, Carapace Press UK.
Swingland (1984) Dietary Preferences of Free Living Chelonians. Symposium on Chelonian Nutrition and Malnutrition, University of Bristol.

Hibernation

Hibernation in Mediterranean tortoises is a response to low environmental temperatures. Tortoises, like all reptiles, are ectotherms that regulate their body temperature by behavioural means. When the surrounding temperatures drop so low that the tortoise is unable to thermoregulate properly, then most Testudo species are able to enter a state of dormancy or relative inactivity to see them through this period.

This is technically called brumation but we know it as hibernation. However not all of the Mediterranean tortoises should be hibernated, in particular those coming from areas that are particularly warm all year round. Such tortoises do not hibernate in the wild and will die if one encourages them in captivity.

Pictured:
A tortoise emerging
from its hibernation bed
of shredded paper.

Species that are safe to hibernate are Testudo graeca ibera, T. g. zarundnyi, T whitei, T. marginata, T. hermanni and T. horsfieldi. Of the T. g. graeca group the Moroccan and Algerian races are safe to hibernate.

Species that should not be hibernated at all are T. kleinmanni and T. nabulensis. The Libyan race of T. g. graeca should either not be hibernated, or only allowed to do so for a relatively short time, such as six to eight weeks, as should T. g. terrestris.

Initiation of hibernation

The major cues for initiating hibernation behaviour begin in late summer/early autumn and really begin to come into force following the autumn equinox. These environmental triggers are:

- Falling ambient temperatures. The days become cooler with lower peak temperatures.

- Shortening day length.

- Reduced daylight intensity. The shorter days and lower position of the sun in the sky mean that any sunlight reaching the tortoise is less intense.

Natural hibernation

Hibernation is a normal physiological event for the majority of Testudo tortoises. Tortoises normally feed well during the late spring and summer, with excess food being converted into fats and sugars that are stored in the body. One important storage substance is glycogen (made from glucose) that is stored in the liver. Fat is also stored in the liver and in the fat pads.

From mid-September onwards the tortoise's behaviour begins to alter. It will spend longer basking and progressively less time eating. By late October to early November it will have ceased feeding altogether in preparation for hibernation. It will, however, have continued to defaecate and urinate as it needs to eliminate as much waste product from its system as possible.

Once ready for hibernation the tortoise will either dig into the ground, or select an appropriate shelter (called a hibernaculum), which in the wild is often a vacated rodent burrow. These hibernacula are often preselected and the tortoise may return to the same place year after year. However, during hibernation, the tortoise is not 'asleep' in the way that we would imagine. The low temperatures mean that their movements are sluggish, but they are still responsive to what is going on around them. For example, the tortoise continues to monitor the surrounding temperature and so, during the winter, as the frost line deepens, the tortoise will dig deeper to avoid it and as temperatures increase it will dig back up towards the surface. At winter temperatures their whole metabolism is turned down to a minimum setting. Their oxygen requirements are minimal and so little overt breathing is needed, but breathe they must, even if it is only occasionally.

Whilst in hibernation the kidneys continue to work, producing small amounts of urine that is stored in the bladder. As the tortoise rarely urinates during hibernation the natural toxins that are normally eliminated in the urine begin to build up in the tortoise's system. One such product, urea, can reach very high levels.

This situation is further worsened because the tortoise gradually dehydrates during hibernation, because it cannot drink, but continually loses tiny amounts of water vapour as it breathes. This further concentrates the urea.

In the American Desert tortoise Gopherus agassizi it has been found that hibernation kills off the natural gut bacterial flora. This therefore needs to be established again the following spring. It is likely that this will also happen in hibernating Mediterranean tortoises.

The end of hibernation

The only trigger for ending hibernation is rising environmental temperatures – hibernating tortoises are underground and so light plays no part. Temperatures over around 10°C (50°F) appear to bring about this 're-awakening'.

To start with the tortoise may just come out and bask for a little while during the day, before digging back in again at night, but eventually a more normal behaviour pattern is resumed.

At the end of hibernation there is a massive release of glucose from the liver glycogen reserves inside the tortoise. This gives the tortoise the energy it needs to feed at a time when its body is carrying very high levels of waste in its system. Waste products such as urea can only be eliminated by urinating and this is why tortoises will pass a large amount of urine within days of arousal. They will drink, if given the opportunity, in order to rehydrate themselves and flush their kidneys through.

Hibernation at home

Under normal weather patterns, late October to early November appears to be the time in the UK when tortoises that are kept outside will begin true hibernation.

Supplementary food should be withheld from around mid-October, or even earlier if the tortoise has access to natural forage. Allowing it to follow a natural feeding pattern is always best.

Tortoises can be allowed to hibernate in several different ways:

Option 1

Should be bullet point allowing the tortoise to select its own spot in the garden and hibernate at liberty. This is the easiest method but is also by far and away the most risky. Tortoises tend to select relatively dry areas such as are found under conifers. This approach has the advantage that the tortoise is in control and there is virtually no input from the owner. The downsides are that there may not truly be any suitable place in your garden – your tortoise will pick the best site that it can but it does not mean that it is perfect.

Your tortoise is also potentially at risk from predators such as rodents and natural catastrophes such as floods, as well as gardeners. Tortoises that hibernate outside are very prone to developing shell rot due to bacterial or fungal infections picked up from the soil.

Option 2

Sinking a bin or other large and deep container into the ground. As a precaution this should have some drainage holes punched in the bottom before it is filled with peat or topsoil and the lid placed back on. As the bin is covered, the soil inside will be dry and the depth of the bin allows the tortoise to naturally adjust its position, according to the soil temperature. This method is better than the first, but the tortoise is still exposed to potential temperature extremes.

Option 3

Indoors in a suitable thermal environment. The ideal temperature for hibernation is around 5 to 6°C (41 to 42.8°F). If the temperature rises above 10°C (50°F) the tortoise begins to 'awaken', whilst temperatures below 0°C (32°F) carry a risk of frost damage. So, a suitable place needs to be selected, such as an unheated outbuilding. Select a smaller container in which your tortoise is to be hibernated. It can be wooden, plastic or polystyrene and should be large enough for your tortoise to move around in. This should then be filled with a suitable insulator such as polystyrene chips, newspaper or straw (if using straw from a bale please make sure there is no baler twine mixed in with it – it can wrap around limbs and cause serious problems). This container should have some air holes in the lid and sides. Then place the whole box is then placed inside a larger container that also contains insulative material in such a way that all sides of the inner box are insulated. Some air holes should be placed in this box too. There is no need to make hundreds of holes as during hibernation the tortoise's oxygen requirements are minimal and will be easily supplied by twelve or so decent sized ventilation holes. During the period of hibernation your tortoise will inevitably dig its way to the bottom of the inner box; with this arrangement it will still be insulated. Remember that the insulative material is not keeping the tortoise warm (the tortoise does not generate any heat), instead it is acting as a buffer against sudden temperature drops outside the box.

Option 4

Refrigerators are increasingly used as hi-tech hibernacula. Temperatures are maintained within the recommended 5 to 6°C (41 to 42.8°F) and opening the door during regular checks should give enough gas exchange for hibernating tortoises.

If in doubt consider removing the sealing from the door. Refrigerators work most effectively in warmer environments - in cold out-buildings the compressor may stop at low temperatures, but your tortoise should still be fine as it is still in a highly insulated box! If necessary temporarily use small bottles of warm water or similar to keep the internal refrigerator temperature correct during severe cold spells.

Monitor the temperature where the tortoise is stored during the winter. If possible, use a max-min thermometer (available from garden supplies) or digital ones(from aquatics outlets or electrical stores) to keep track of temperature variations.

Tortoises should be checked prior to hibernation and their weight recorded. This is because they lose weight during hibernation. On average expect a loss of around 1% body weight per month, so regular weighing helps you to monitor the tortoise's health during hibernation. Providing the tortoise is not exposed to high temperatures it will not be disturbed from its hibernation by handling and weighing, although they will often hiss whilst being handled. If the weight loss is approaching 8 to 10% per month then the tortoise must be awakened.

Tortoises are not 'asleep' as such during hibernation

and will move around, as they would do in the wild, especially if they sense a drop or rise in temperature. This does not mean that they are 'waking up, and should not be taken out of hibernation unless the temperature is correct to do so. When temperatures start to rise consistently over 10°C (50°F), the tortoise will start to become more active. This is the time to bring it out of hibernation. Give your tortoise a shallow, luke warm bath, which will allow it to drink and encourage urination.

Healthy tortoises should be drinking well within a week of coming out of hibernation and eating within two weeks. If they are not it is important that you seek veterinary attention.

Unsuitable hibernation techniques

Hibernation is something that we humans do not do and because we have no experience of it, many new owners are concerned and believe that there are significant risks involved for their tortoise. However, providing the tortoise is of the right species and is healthy, hibernation is a normal behaviour and should be encouraged.

It is also true that many tortoises do well without being hibernated, although this may, long term, increase the risk of hepatic lipidosis, especially in older females. To safely hibernate a tortoise should be exposed to the environmental triggers as outlined above. A decision should be made in the midsummer to early autumn as to whether your tortoise should be hibernated.

The worst possible scenario is to adopt a middle option where the tortoise is 'hibernated' somewhere that is unsuitable, typically that is too warm. These tortoises may not be offered food or water (because they're thought to be hibernating) or be unwilling to eat or drink (because their internal clock says they should be dormant, but its just too warm). Unsuitable situations I've encountered are tortoises kept by the Aga/radiator in winter (too warm/abnormal daylength from artificial room lighting), in bedrooms (too warm/too light) or even in cupboards under the stairs (too warm). In each of these situations the tortoises remain more active then they should be and use up vital energy reserves without replacing them by feeding. Failure to drink will exacerbate the naturally occurring dehydration. Such tortoises are more prone to post-hibernational anorexia than those that have been correctly cared for.

Keeping tortoises awake through the winter

Those tortoises listed above as inappropriate to hibernate, or those which have been unwell and for whom hibernation may be dangerous, will need to be kept awake throughout the winter. To do this you will need a suitable vivarium. To try to keep your tortoise awake you need to remove or reverse the natural environmental cues for hibernation. Ideally this should begin before the autumn equinox. You can try to convince the tortoise that it is a Mediterranean summer by providing:

1. High temperatures, with a hot spot that allows the tortoise to achieve a preferred body temperature of 30°C (86°F).

2. 14 hours of daylight that is provided by full spectrum lighting. Use two or three tubes to give summer intensity.

However, some tortoises seem to follow their own internal clock no matter what we do. In these cases allow a short hibernation of four weeks, and then reawaken and place in a vivarium as described above.

Post-hibernational Anorexia

A post-hibernational anorexia is when the tortoise awakens from hibernation but refuses to feed. There are several possible causes of this, but typically it is due to inadequate preparation the previous year with insufficient storage of fat.

Once the tortoise has used up its entire fat and glycogen reserves (and so also exhausting its fat soluble vitamin stores) it is forced to breakdown muscle and other body proteins as alternative energy and amino acid sources. Unfortunately, this increased protein metabolism causes an increase in urea production which, at a time when levels are naturally high, forces the urea levels up to dangerous levels that can suppress the immune system of the tortoise, depress appetite and stop the kidneys from working properly. The result is that these tortoises have no stored glycogen left to fuel their foraging. This means that blood sugar levels are very low and so they start on a downward spiral of further protein breakdown, which leads to higher urea levels and so on. The poor immunity of these animals also leave them open to secondary bacterial infections, especially stomatitis (mouth rot) and septicaemia.

Pictured:
Checking the inside of your tortoise's mouth is often not as easy as this.

Treatment can be prolonged, and your veterinary surgeon may need to do blood tests and other investigations to find out what is going on inside your tortoise. As a general rule treatment involves:

1. Correcting any dehydration. Initially try regular baths and if, after a couple of days, the tortoise is not drinking then fluid may need to be given by stomach tube. Use an oral rehydration preparation. This is normally given at around 2 to 4% bodyweight per day e.g. if the tortoise weighs 1.0 kg = 1000 g, then 2% would be 20 mls. This is given divided into 2 or 3 doses each day. It cannot be overstated that correcting the dehydration (which will reduce the blood urea levels and so encourage urination) is crucial to the recovery of the tortoise. Always start at the lower dose rate until you become proficient at this technique.

2. Vitamins should be given either by mouth or by injection, as the tortoise will have very low levels.

3. Place the tortoise into a vivarium as described for 'Keeping Tortoises Awake through the Winter'. UVA in particular will help to trigger normal behaviour including feeding.

4. Stomach tube the tortoise with a suitable food replacement. This simple procedure is best demonstrated by someone experienced such as your veterinarian.

Initially try a soluble replacement product such as VetArk's Critical Care, and then move on to the supportive products available for herbivorous animals such as Critical Care (Oxbow) or Recovery Diet (Supreme Pet Foods). These can be made up into a suspension and tubed. If these are not available then baby foods (vegetable based without milk or milk products) are a useful alternative. Feeding should be done initially twice weekly. In some cases your vet may suggest an indwelling oesophagostomy tube – a tube inserted through the side of the neck and into the stomach with the free end attached to the carapace. It sounds horrendous but it can be life-saving!

5. Mix a probiotic with the food. These safe bacterial cultures will help to recolonise the possibly sterile gut of the tortoise, helping it towards normal feeding and digestion.

6. Any specific disease conditions, for example stomatitis, should be treated. Your tortoise should be checked for blindness that can be caused by cataracts - sometimes these form after exposure to excessively low temperatures during hibernation.

7. Keep going! Some tortoises will take weeks, even months, before they will start to feed normally.

Shell rot

Tortoises allowed to hibernate in the soil outside are particularly prone to this, as soil-bourne organisms – both bacteria and fungi – invade and establish in the keratin of the scutes. The scutes become pitted and flaky and in some cases the overlying keratin comes away and the underlying bone is exposed. Treatment involves removal of as much of the loose and flakey material as possible and regular cleaning of the affected areas with a topical iodine solution. In the worst cases the infected scutes may need to be removed. This can be very painful for the tortoise and so it may need to be done under a general anaesthetic, and antibiotics or antifungals may need to be given.

Making more tortoises

Tortoises do not live in tight social groups and this relatively solitary existence means that meetings between males and females are uncommon and so are opportunities for mating. As a result, sexually mature tortoises (especially males) will mate whenever the opportunity arises. This helps to explain much of their behaviour in that male tortoises are sexually promiscuous and will attempt to mate with as many females as possible, whilst driving away other males. This benefits the males by maximising their chances of fertilising as many eggs as possible.

Pictured:
Captive breeding is
no longer as rare as
it once was.

In contast females, on the other hand, which are ready for breeding will appear to play hard to get, often leading the male on a prolonged 'chase'. During this 'courtship' the male will attempt to butt the female with the front of his shell and it may be that this, and his ability to keep up with her, allows her to assess his health and strength and so his fitness to father her young. Producing eggs is energetically expensive and so must not be wasted on a second rate male, but instead must be with the best she can get! Female tortoises are able to store sperm from a single mating for several months so that a single mating may provide enough sperm to fertilise several clutches of eggs.

Courtship can appear quite traumatic with seemingly nasty males trailing and biting at exposed parts of the female. This is normal, and is probably a significant stimulus, triggering ovulation to occur. In the limited space of an enclosure however, serious damage can occur if the female cannot escape the attention of an over-amorous male.

Often the first indication of mating behaviour is the clacking sound of shell against shell as the male bashes the front of his shell against that of the female – a sure sign of attempted courtship.

This behaviour is designed to stop the female from escaping, rather than actively repulse her. Eventually the male will make his way to the back of the female and attempt to mount – in some species this is aided by the concavity of the male's plastron, allowing him to fit better on the back of the female's carapace. The male will attempt to engage his phallus with her cloaca whilst the female will assist this by extending her back legs to lift her cloaca as far off the ground as possible. In some species this is almost a reflex – for example, female Hermann's tortoises will respond to pressure on the back half of the carapace by lifting their back end up. During copulation the male may vocalise.

Egg laying

In the wild, the adult females of most of the species of Mediterranean tortoises will lay between one and three clutches of eggs per year. Each clutch will contain between two and twelve eggs on average, the number depending upon the age and size of the female. An exception to this is the Egyptian tortoise T. kleinmanii. These females lay only one, occasionally two eggs, at a time. This occurs at monthly intervals, until four or five eggs have been laid in total, before entering a resting phase of a few months.

The time between mating to egg laying is variable, because of the ability of the female to store sperm, and can vary from eight weeks to well over two years. Ovulation, with the release of a viable egg from the ovary into the female reproductive tract depends upon a number of factors, some of which are internal and some that are external. One of the main factors to trigger ovulation is the presence of a sexually active male and active courtship. Pheromones will also play a significant part.

Once a clutch of eggs is ready the female will choose a suitable site to lay their eggs based upon a number of factors such as soil texture, but the overriding feature is temperature. She is looking for a place where the eggs can be incubated at around 25 to 30°C (77 to 86°F) for some eight to twelve weeks, so the surface of the egg deposition site must be warm enough. She will test the temperature by sniffing the selected area and she may dig several scrapes, again testing the subsurface temperature, with her hind legs first, before finally deciding upon the best spot. If there is nowhere deemed suitable, some females may not lay their eggs. In these cases the eggs just sit in the reproductive tract, eventually causing problems. Occasionally, extra shells are laid down on such eggs, bulking them out to a size where they can no longer be passed.

When egg-laying begins the female will scoop out a hole into which the clutch is laid. Once the full clutch is dropped into the hole, the eggs are covered. The female plays no more part in the care of her eggs or young after this point.

Suggestions for providing breeding females with suitable nesting conditions is given by Highfield (2002). These are:

- A gentle slope, preferably facing south.

- The substrate should be of sandy, well-drained soil. Often a mixture of play sand (60%) and loamy compost (40%) is accepted.

- The site should be dry and in full sun. Mediterranean tortoises will usually lay during the afternoon on warm, sunny days.

- There should be adequate depth of substrate. As a rough guide this should be at least equal to the length of the hind legs plus 70% the length of the carapace.

- Indoor nesting sites these should be around one square metre, with the surface heated by a basking lamp.

Temperature-dependant sex determination

In all chelonians so far studied, sex determination of the embryos is not chromosomal as seen in mammals and birds, but appears to be due to the incubation temperature the embryo is exposed to at a critical point of its development.

This Temperature-Dependant Sex Determination (TDSD) is mediated by certain genes being either switched on or turned off at certain temperatures. It is the proteins and enzymes triggered by these genes that eventually lead to the embryo becoming either male or female. It is still not known to what benefit TDSD has in the wild, but in captivity it can be used to our advantage, because by altering the incubation temperature we can skew the proportions of males to females to suit.

In general, the higher incubation temperatures favour females, whilst lower temperatures tend to produce males. In both T. hermanni and T. graeca temperatures of 25 to 30°C (77 to 86°F) usually produce males whilst 31 to 35°C (87.8 to 95°F) generates more females.

Practical incubation

In the United Kingdom and other northern hemisphere countries, soil temperature is usually inadequate for normal incubation to occur outside, so we must incubate them artificially. Fortunately tortoise eggs, unlike bird eggs, do not need to be turned, so this makes using an incubator relatively straightforward.

Commercial reptile incubators and incubator kits are available, but should you wish to make your own then any heat resistant container will do. The necessary heat source can be a small light bulb, a ceramic heater or a vivarium heat mat that is connected to an accurate thermostat. The temperature probe of the thermostat should be laid next to the eggs. An accurate thermometer is also required (to double check on the accuracy of the thermostat), plus a hygrometer to measure humidity. These are available from garden centres and specialist reptile outlets. The incubator must not be permanently sealed, as some air exchange is necessary, even if this is only by lifting the lid once daily to check on the eggs. Use a small container, such as an old clean margarine tub and place some clean sand, earth or vermiculite (available from garden centres) as a substrate into this tub. Then, place each egg into the substrate in such a way to create a shallow depression. The eggs should not be touching and they do not need to be buried. Place a card or other label with the species and date of lay in the same tub.

Temperature is crucial, especially with regard to TDSD. Humidity less so for hard-shelled Testudo species, but an excessively low humidity can lead to the eggs desiccating. If you are not trying to influence sex, adjust the temperature to 30 to 31°C (86 to 87.8°F) and aim for a humidity of 70 to 80%.

Incubation times

The incubation lengths given in Table 2 (below) are guides only as they can vary considerably depending upon the temperature of incubation (lower temperatures produce longer incubation times). Occasionally some eggs within a clutch may exhibit diapause, where there is a temporary halt in embryonic development, often at the early stages. This may be an adaptive process to stagger the hatching of young over a period of time, possibly to reduce the risk of exposing all of a given brood to unfavourable environmental conditions.

Species	Temperature (°C)	Incubation length (days)
Hermann's Tortoise (Testudo hermanni)	25– 28 (77– 82.4°F)	75– 80
	30– 31 (86– 87.8°F)	56– 63
Spur-thighed tortoise (Testudo graeca)	25– 26 (77– 78.8°F)	75– 80
	30– 31 (86– 87.8°F)	56– 63
Spur-thighed tortoise (Testudo graeca ibera)	30 (86°F)	56– 65
Marginated tortoise (Testudo marginata)	25– 26 (77– 78.8°F)	75– 80
	30– 31 (86– 87.8°F)	56– 63
Horsfield's tortoise (Testudo horsfieldi)	30– 31 (86– 87.8°F)	61– 75

Infertility

Tortoises may be infertile for a variety of reasons, including immaturity and underlying disease, but sometimes their eggs do not develop because the nutrition of the adults is poor. Captive-produced Hermann's tortoise eggs have been shown to be have yolks that are low in docosahexaenoic acid and vitamin A levels, both of which are essential for the developing embryo. It is thought that adult diets low in these substances, or in their precursors (alphalinolenic acid and beta-carotene) will result in deficiencies in the yolks and hence failure of tortoise embryos to develop. Feeding red, yellow or orange vegetables such as carrots or peppers will help to counter this.

Failure to hatch/
dead-in-shell

There are many reasons why tortoise eggs do not hatch, but typical problem issues are:

1. **Temperature.** Temperatures too high or too low can cause embryonic death.

2. **Humidity.** Tortoise eggs are relatively resistant to poor humidity levels, which is probably why so many people have managed to hatch eggs in airing cupboards! Humidity should be monitored however and if possible maintained at 70 to 80%. A very low humidity, or a high airflow over the eggs can lead to too much evaporative water loss from the eggs causing dehydration and embryonic death. An egg that loses 25% or more of its weight during incubation is unlikely to hatch.

3. **Oxygen and carbon dioxide levels.** Remember that a developing tortoise inside the egg needs to breathe. This it does not through its lungs but across the eggshell. On the inside of the shell are membranes well supplied with blood vessels that pick up oxygen from air in microscopic holes in the shell and disperse carbon dioxide the same way.

In sealed containers oxygen levels may fall and carbon dioxide levels rise to dangerous levels. Briefly opening such incubators once daily or every other day will prevent this from happening.

Once an egg is laid and has come to rest, the embryo (which at this stage consists of only an aggregate of cells) gradually migrates up to the highest point on the inside of the shell such that it eventually comes to sit on top of the yolk. After 24 to 48 hours it attaches to the inner cell membrane (the allantois). This membrane is important for oxygen uptake and carbon dioxide release, calcium absorption from the shell and storage of harmful waste products. This connection is vital to the embryo but is, to start with, very fragile. Any rotation of the egg from around 24 hours after laying to around 20 days of incubation is liable to sheer off the embryo and cause its death.

When handling eggs always be careful not to rotate them, and if removing eggs from natural egg sites to place into incubators always try to do it within 24 hours of laying (before the embryo has attached) and mark the top of each egg with a permanent marker pen or similar so that you always know the orientation.

Candling

Candling involves shining a very bright light through the egg to see if it is fertile. If there is a sizeable embryo present it will be seen as a shadow. Often such a shadow is not visible until almost the end of incubation – possibly because it is only by this point that the developing tortoise is dense enough to block any light. Blood vessels on the inside of the shell may also be visible.

Hatching

As incubation progresses the shell becomes thinner in patches as calcium is absorbed from the outer calcified layer and transferred into the skeleton of the developing tortoise. At the end of incubation the tortoise will hatch. The hatchling tortoise forms a small "egg tooth" on its nose and it uses this to wear its way through the shell until it begins to crack. Often once the shell is punctured and a small chip is displaced, then the tortoise may take a rest, but eventually the tortoise will be able to climb out of the shell. The hatchling tortoise is a perfect miniature of the adult. Many hatchlings will appear to be bent over – a necessity inside the confines of the egg – but over the next twenty-four hours or so they will gradually straighten out. Occasionally, some hatching tortoises will appear to have trouble getting out of their shell. It is tempting to help them, but be careful. Hatchlings often have large yolk sacs that still have not been absorbed, and the blood vessels lining the inside of the shell are still functional. It is very easy to damage these structures with a serious risk of fatal haemorrhage or wounding.

Hatchling aftercare

Newly hatched tortoises still have an internal yolk sac to supply them with food for the first few days. However, it is better to offer food sooner rather than later. Feed shredded pieces of green foods plus a calcium supplement. Also, bathe the tortoise every day to encourage it to drink.

Hatchling tortoises need to be kept in vivaria. It is particularly important to provide hiding places for hatchling and young tortoises. At this age they have many predators and in the wild and they will instinctively appreciate cover; behaviour that will also lead them into appropriate microclimates that help them to survive. Hatchling tortoises will appreciate such hides and the chances are that your well-adjusted babies will soon learn where the food comes from and will readily greet you at the front of their vivarium.

Pictured:
There are few things cuter than a baby tortoise.

Reproduction:
related
problems

Egg-binding

Any adult female tortoise that shows non-specific signs of ill health, restlessness or persistent straining should be assessed for egg-binding (dystocia). There are two forms:

Follicular stasis

The eggs develop on the ovaries, but are not ovulated. The ovaries eventually become overloaded with retained yolks, forming into large pendulous masses, which take up a significant amount of space in the body cavity. This can be diagnosed either on ultrasound scanning or by endoscopy and may be associated with low thyroid levels. It can also sometimes be triggered in females that have sudden contact with males after years, or even decades without access to other tortoises. Typical examples are when owners 'tortoise sit' for other people, resulting in two single tortoises suddenly, being thrust together. It may be that the physical presence and activity of the male, plus pheromones produced by him trigger ovarian activity, but full ovulation does not occur.

Post-ovulatory egg retention (true egg-binding)

Here eggs that are shelled to varying degrees are present within the oviducts. It is easily diagnosed by x-rays as the shells show up readily. Possible causes for this include environmental (e.g. no provision of suitable egg deposition sites), low calcium levels, fractured or deformed pelvis, internal tumours and so on ,so your veterinarian may need to do several tests to investigate the problem. Treatment of simple post-ovulatory dystocia involves calcium and oxytocin injections. If these fail to work, then removal of the eggs via a surgical flap created in the plastron is advised, possibly accompanied by an ovaro-hysterectomy.

Prolapsed phallus

This is where the male is unable to retract his phallus, and overtime it becomes progressively more damaged by his dragging it along the ground and catching it with his feet and claws. Rarely it can be a lack of calcium and in others it is due to damage to the muscle that pulls the phallus back into the cloaca. This damage can occur during mating. Treatment may involve antibiotics and surgical replacement; in others amputation of the phallus is needed.

As the male tortoise does not urinate through his phallus this surgery will only affect his ability to mate.

References

Highfield A.C 2002 Natural and Artificial Nest sites for Terrestrial Tortoises in Tortoise Trust Newsletter Number 3 & 4 pp 19 - 20.

In sickness
& in health

Routine health checks ought to be performed on each of your tortoises on a regular basis. How often is up to you, but they can easily be incorporated into the routine examination that is carried out both before and after hibernation.

The before (pre-) hibernation health check should, in the UK, be done in early to mid- September, the tortoise begins to wind down for hibernation. By doing this relatively early it gives us a chance to either sort out minor problems before hibernation, or establish a suitable vivarium if the tortoise is to be kept awake over the winter. The check after hibernation (post-hibernation) should be done within two to three weeks after your tortoise emerges. By this stage your tortoise should be eating and drinking normally. If it is not then further investigations may be needed.

Pictured:
A healthy tortoise
should appear alert,
with no nasal discharge.

Routine Checks

Weight to length ratio. This ratio is an attempt to gauge the bodily condition of the tortoise by comparing two easily measured factors – its weight and its carapacial length. Typically this is displayed on a graph with three lines marked on it – the upper and lower limits of normal, plus the average. Tortoises in poor condition will often fall below the lower line, whilst obese tortoises will be way above the average. For hatchling and young tortoises weight and length checks should be done frequently, for example at monthly intervals, to monitor growth.

Many tortoises grow in a series of growth spurts and this may be reflected in your findings. Weight loss however is often the first indicator of a possible problem even if the tortoise appears otherwise well.

There ratios are species-specific. The original one, sometimes known as the Jackson ratio after the veterinary surgeon, Oliphant Jackson FRCVS, who first published this simple procedure, applies only toHerman's tortoises Testudo hermanii and the spurthighed group (T. graeca) and is reasonably valid for the species and subspecies that make up this group. It is not appropriate for Testudo horsfieldi, T. kleinmanni, T. marginata and Furculachelys nabulensis.

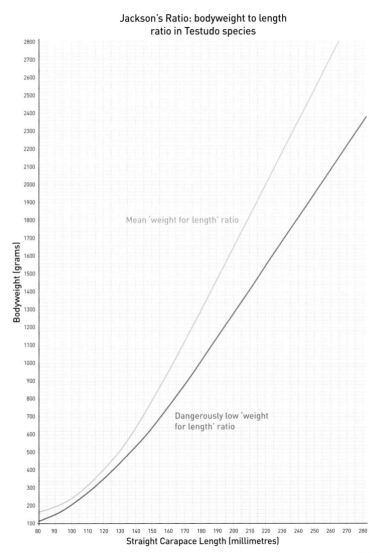

Jackson's Ratio: bodyweight to length ratio in Testudo species

Bodyweight (grams)

Straight Carapace Length (millimetres)

Mean 'weight for length' ratio

Dangerously low 'weight for length' ratio

It probably does not apply to Testudo whitei, although it is possible that some may have been included in the original work as mis-identified T. graeca. Recently a similar ratio has been evaluated for Horsfield's tortoise T. horsfieldi by J.S. Craig, and is known as the McIntyre ratio. (Opposite)

For these ratios weight is measured in grams. Try to use scales that weigh to the nearest gram, although the nearest 5g is acceptable for large tortoises. Many tortoises will not keep still on a scales but do not be afraid to turn your tortoise on its back

for the few seconds necessary to get an accurate weight; it will come to no harm.

The length is a straight, linear measurement from the most forward point of the carapace to the most hind point. It is not measured over the top of the carapace. If you measure this way then you will get an erroneously long length and the tortoise will appear underweight on the graph. The length is measured in millimetres.

Although the weight to length ratio is a useful indicator, do not get too hung up on it. It has a limited use because, not only is it species specific, as outlined above, but also does not take into account the different shape of the carapace between the sexes.

McIntyre Ratio for Horsfields' Tortoise

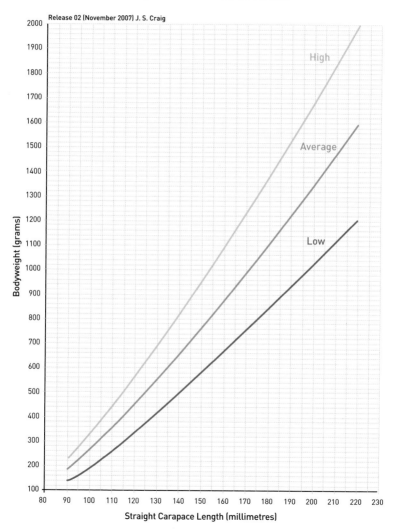

Release 02 (November 2007) J. S. Craig

Male tortoises tend to have a flatter carapace than females, which in turn tend to be more domed. This means that females are often significantly heavier, whilst healthy males can regularly come in either on or just below the 'minimum' line.

This does not mean that if you have these species you should not bother to take these measurements – in fact quite the contrary because as the years go by this historical information can prove invaluable, providing a database of normal values, especially if your tortoise becomes unwell.

Alternatively for Herman's tortoises Testudo hermanii and the spur-thighed group (T. graeca) there is a mathematical formula that can applied. Here the weight of the tortoise in grams is divided by the cube of the straight length of the carapace (measured in centimetres). The resulting ratio is compared to the straight length of the carapace. Note that again the straight length of the carapace is a linear measurement from the most forward point of the carapace to the furthest back and is not a measurement over the dome of the carapace.

Straight length of carapace	Normal Ratio
> 15cm	0.21– 0.23
< 15cm	0.23– 0.25

Tortoises with a ratio of 0.17 or less are considered critical., whilst examples for tortoises with a high ratio are obesity (hepatic lipidosis) or pregnancy (multiple eggs, averaging around 10g each).

For Horsfield's tortoises, a formula that has been used is:

Carapace length (cm) x carapace height (cm)
x carapace width (cm) x 0.57 = weight (g).

This would appear to be of limited value as no indication is given of how obese or underweight your tortoise is relative to established normal values.

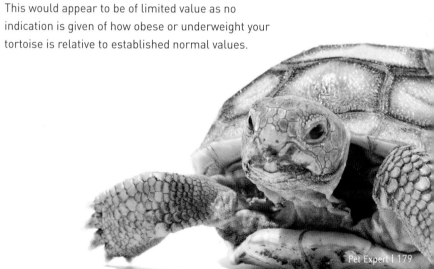

Overall health check

Give each tortoise a thorough examination, checking not only its shell but its limbs, head, neck and tail for any lesions or, in particular, swellings that may indicate an abscess. Eyes should be bright and there should be no discharge from the eyes, nose or mouth. Your veterinary surgeon will be able to give a more thorough check including an ophthalmic examination.

If your tortoise is not microchipped then photocopying or photographing the plastron on an annual basis will record any changes to keep an up to date record for identification purposes.

Worming

As a routine this also works well twice yearly. In particular the post-hibernation worming will help to kill off adult worms before they start producing eggs.

Health Care

Tortoises can be hardy animals providing they are healthy and well cared for. However, as with all animals, some do become ill for a variety of reasons. If your tortoise becomes unwell then it is probably best kept in a vivarium. Hygiene is important –

use only newspaper on the bottom so that it can be cleaned out easily as soon as it is soiled, and make sure that any vivarium furniture such as hides can either be sterilised or thrown away once your tortoise is well again. Wooden objects in particular can harbour bugs and bacteria and are difficult to clean properly. Other considerations are that your tortoise should be in a stress free environment; that it should be at the correct temperature and that it should be well hydrated. The latter can often be achieved by daily baths. Use a cat litter tray or similar and add luke warm water to the level of the junction between the carapace and the plastron. Bathing allows the tortoise to drink easily and often encourages it to defaecate and urinate.

A number of diseases and disorders have already been discussed where relevant under previous chapters. The rest of this chapter will cover other common problems seen in pet tortoises.

Runny Nose Syndrome (RNS)

RNS is a common condition in pet tortoises that at present should be considered as a symptom rather than a disease. Often it is mild and the tortoise may show no signs of ill health, but it can be linked to a debilitating condition. Classic diseases causing RNS include chelonian herpesvirus and mycoplasmas (see under individual headings), but in some cases RNS can be linked to general poor health, unsuitable environment or problems that are not immediately obvious, for example an internal abscess. An investigation into RNS may involve your veterinarian submitting nasal

discharge from your tortoise for laboratory investigation to look for chelonian herpes virus and mycoplasma DNA, bacteriological culture as well as blood samples and radiographs.

Viral Diseases

Chelonian Herpesvirus (CHV). This is a serious viral disease of tortoises and is a common cause of Runny Nose Syndrome.

Tortoises with CHV show a persistent nasal discharge that can vary from clear and watery to thick and mucousy. There appears to be an accompanying immune suppression and infected tortoises often have recurring parasitic infestations (especially with flagellates). Appetite generally remains good but diarrhoea is common. In some cases the infection progresses and the tortoise becomes anaemic. This is often associated with other internal organs becoming diseased. These tortoises can become jaundiced and death can follow, often as a result of a secondary mouth infections, pneumonia or kidney failure. Treatment with the human anti-herpesvirus

medication acyclovir has been suggested but not proven as an effective medication.

It is thought that Testudo graeca ibera may be an asymptommatic carrier of at CHV, with deaths in mixed collections being mostly confined to the North African Spurthighed tortoise Testudo g.graeca.

Bacterial Diseases

Abscesses are very common in tortoises, but unlike in mammals, reptilian pus is rarely liquid but is more often thick, cheese-like material. Surrounding the abscess is a thick fibrous capsule that makes antibiotic penetration difficult, so surgery is often resorted to effect a cure. Where limbs, joints or extremities such as the nose are affected, then radiography should be performed to check for signs of infection in the underlying bone.

Tympanic (ear) abscesses

Tympanic (ear) abscesses show as bulging of the tympanic scale on one or both sides. These are often secondary to a bacterial mouth infection (stomatitis) with infection ascending the Eustachian tube into the middle ear cavity.

Ear abscesses are quite common, and may in some cases be linked with gastro-intestinal worms.

Management of all abscesses is similar, involving the combination of appropriate antibiotics and surgical removal of pus.

Stomatitis (or mouth rot)

Stomatitis (or mouth rot) is occasionally encountered especially after hibernation. Inside the mouth one may see inflammation, blood or whitish plaques on the tongue, back of the mouth and hard palate. Bacterial infections usually play a significant role, although viral and fungal causes can sometimes be found. Following swabbing for routine bacterial culture, cleaning up the mouth is necessary. In severe cases this potentially painful procedure should be done under a general anaesthetic. Antibiotics or antifungals should be used depending upon the cause. Chelonia with stomatitis will not eat or drink voluntarily.

Septicaemia

Septicaemia presents as haemorrhages in the skin and in the shell. In severe cases fluid may accumulate beneath the keratin shields of the shell. Jaundicing may be seen. Antibiotics and fluid support is essential in these cases.

Salmonella

There is often concern about the risk of contracting Salmonella from tortoises, but infections from chelonia are relatively rare and are usually due to a breakdown in hygiene and poor husbandry, allowing an environmental build up. As a general rule pregnant women, children less than five years of age and persons with impaired immune system function (e.g. HIV positive or undertaking chemotherapy) should not have contact with reptiles.

Mycoplasmas

These are bacteria-like organisms that cause inflammation of the nasal cavity and around the eyes producing a typical RNS picture. Symptoms are similar to that seen with CHV. Infection can be long term and in some individuals no symptoms may be visible.

Parasites

Flagellates are single-celled parasites and infestations. Often they are present in cases of gastro-intestinal disease linked with a loss of appetite. Affected tortoises will void large quantities of watery diarrhoea. Examination of such faeces under a light microscope will reveal huge numbers of these motile protozoa.

Although they can be considered as normal inhabitants of the gut fauna, in large numbers they are pathogenic. In many cases they are secondary opportunists so the possibility of a concurrent disease should be considered. Treatment is with metronidazole prescribed by your veterinarian. Occasionally the protozoan Hexamita may be a cause of kidney disease.

Worms

Around 30 to 40% of tortoises carry nematode infestations, usually Tachygonetria species. Other species found include Sulcascaris and Angusticaecum.

Tachygonetria worms are particular parasites of Testudo species. Several different species of these worms can be found living naturally in the intestine of wild tortoises and it is thought that here they may be beneficial, helping to churn over the gut contents andbreak it down to aid bacterial degradation. In captivity however any stress on the tortoise such as poor diet or living conditions can tip the balance in favour of the worms. Large infestations will compete for the host's food, and can cause blockages.

Angusticaecum are large worms. The larval stages migrate through the body and can cause disease in a variety of organ systems.

The life cycle of most worms is believed to be indirect (though they have not been worked out) but Angusticaecum can have a direct life cycle. Its eggs can survive for months and can certainly over winter outside to re-infect the tortoise the following spring. Regular worming twice yearly is to be recommended. This is best undertaken by your veterinarian during pre- and post-hibernation checks.

A common situation that appears to arise is where owners gradually take on a number of tortoises over successive years. Over this period worm numbers and the egg burden in the soil will progressively builds up to such a level that worms become a serious problem. Often worms appear to become a 'sudden' problem, and may be seen in the faeces and occasionally inside the mouth. Such have not come in from outside, on food or in birds but have just passed a numerical threshold where their presence becomes obvious.

Fly strike

Occasionally fly larvae (maggots) may be seen after flies have laid eggs on faecal-stained areas. Not surprisingly this can occur especially around the cloaca. Any eggs or larvae should be removed as quickly as possible and the area cleaned up with an iodine based wash. Seek veterinary attention as soon as possible.

Ticks are rarely encountered except on wild caught chelonia. They ought to be removed individually. Be aware that abscesses can arise at tick attachment sites.

Note: The parasiticide Ivermectin should never be used with tortoises as it regularly causes fatalities.

Gout

Tortoises eliminate most of their waste nitrogen as uric acid which is seen as the white crystals typical of normal urine. In cases of kidney disease or severe dehydration, when urination ceases or is much reduced, uric acid can crystallize out in the kidneys causing serious renal damage. Uric acid crystals can also form in other organs and in the joints as well, causing the condition known as gout. This is a serious condition and can prove fatal. Gout is a common consequence of many disease processes in tortoises because once the tortoise stops eating and drinking there is an ever-increasing risk of gout occuring.

Bladder stones are a particular problem with young tortoises. Often it is as a result of prolonged mild dehydration such as seen where the tortoises do not have access to a humid microclimate (under branches or hides). Uric acid crystals form in the bladder and these trigger more to form until a stone is produced.

These stones can act as a focus for infection and cause cystitis. Often these stones are passed out eventually, with some straining on the part of the tortoise. In some cases the blad er stone is too big to be voided and surgery may be needed, or medication in the form of allopurinol to stop the further formation of more uric acid. Bladders stones usually show up well on radiographs.

Drowning

Tortoises are generally poor swimmers and can (and do!) fall into unprotected ponds and streams. The position of the lungs in the top part of the carapace mean that they can survive underwater for some time, but should this happen to your tortoise you must seek immediate veterinary attention. First aid can be undertaken by working all four of the limbs of the tortoise in and out of the shell to compress the lungs, whilst holding the tortoise upside down. This may help to void excess water from the lungs. Tortoises submerged for long periods of time absorb large volumes of water and diuretics may need to be administered to help the tortoise eliminate this excess.

Inhalation of water will lead on to pneumonia so antibiotics are often needed.

More information

Tortoise organisations

Great Britain

British Chelonia Group:
www.britishcheloniagroup.org.uk
Tortoise Trust: www.tortoisetrust.org
In addition to the website, Tortoise Trust produce a
number of excellent publications.

Ireland

Irish Association of Tortoise Keepers:
http://homepage.tinet.ie/~090316

Italy

Carapax: www.carapax.org

France

Le Village de Tortues: www.villagetortues.com

USA

New York Turtle and Tortoise Society:
www.nytts.org
American Tortoise Rescue: www.tortoise.com
Gulf coast Turtle and Tortoise Society: www.gctts.org
Mid Atlantic Turtle and Tortoise Association
www.matts-turtles.org

International

World Chelonian Trust: www.chelonia.org

Further reading

Tortoise by Peter Young. Published in 2003 by
Reaktion Books Ltd, 79 Farringdon Road, London
EC1M 3JU. ISBN 1-88189-191-1. Not a tortoise
manual but a fascinating overview of our relationship
to tortoises.

The Tortoise Trust Guide to Tortoises and Turtles
(3rd Edition) by A.C. Highfield. Published in 2004 by
Carapace Press, London. ISBN 1-873943-88-1
5 800040 117271

Units & measures

If you prefer your units in fahrenheit and inches, you can use this conversion chart:

Length in inches	Length in cm	Temperature in °C	Temperature in °F
1	2.5	10	50
2	5.1	15	59
3	7.6	20	68
4	10.2	25	77
5	12.7	30	86
8	20.3	35	95
10	25.4	40	104
15	38.1	45	113

Measurements rounded to 1 decimal place.